PSYCHOLOGY OF LIVING BOOKS:
A SERIES OF TOOLS FOR GROWTH

LAURIE and JOSEPH BRAGA, *general editors*
University of Miami Medical School

PSYCHOLOGY OF LIVING BOOKS is a series of tools for growth, based on current research in psychology and the other sciences of human behavior. The books offer practical information and techniques with which readers can examine their own and others' behavior patterns and underlying needs and motivations. Through these resources and insights, readers can constructively gain understanding of themselves and others as well as the means for change.

Help Your Baby Learn offers practical information and techniques through which you can learn to recognize babies' needs and help them grow as you grow in understanding. STEPHEN LEHANE is on the faculty of the Department of Early Childhood Education at Kent State University, Kent, Ohio.

Also Under the Editorship of Drs. Braga

Children and Adults: Activities for Growing Together
by Joseph and Laurie Braga
Death: The Final Stage of Growth by Elisabeth Kübler-Ross
Learning and Growing: A Guide to Child Development,
by Laurie and Joseph Braga
Growing Older, by Margaret Hellie Huyck
Growing with Children, by Joseph and Laurie Braga
Culture and Human Development, by Ashley Montagu

HELP YOUR BABY LEARN

100 Piaget-Based Activities
For the First Two Years
Of Life

STEPHEN LEHANE

Department of Education
Duke University
Durham, North Carolina

A SPECTRUM BOOK

PRENTICE-HALL, INC.
Englewood Cliffs, New Jersey

Library of Congress Cataloging in Publication Data

Lehane, Stephen.
  Help your baby learn.

  (Psychology of living) (A Spectrum Book)
  Bibliography: p.
  1. Infant psychology.   2. Cognition (Child psychology)
3. Perceptual-motor learning.   4. Play.   I. Title.
BF723.I6L35   649′.122′019   76-5830
ISBN 0-13-386326-3
ISBN 0-13-386318-2 pbk.

© 1976 by Stephen Lehane

Cover photograph by Richard Schwartz

A Spectrum Book

10   9   8   7   6   5

Printed in the United States of America

Prentice-Hall International, Inc., *London*
Prentice-Hall of Australia Pty. Limited, *Sydney*
Prentice-Hall of Canada, Ltd., *Toronto*
Prentice-Hall of India Private Limited, *New Delhi*
Prentice-Hall of Japan, Inc., *Tokyo*
Prentice-Hall of Southeast Asia Pte. Ltd., *Singapore*

To

IDA, FRANK, NINA, JO, AND TOM

CONTENTS

Stage 4

DEVELOPING TOOLS
(EIGHT TO FOURTEEN MONTHS)

Stage 5

EXPERIMENTING
(TWELVE TO TWENTY MONTHS)

FOREWORD

Children's early years are the foundation on which the rest of their experiences are built. In these years, they learn the basics of the skills that make them uniquely human. They learn to move on two legs. They learn to use their hands as tools, and they learn to use their hands to use tools (e.g., eating utensils, writing implements). They learn to use language to communicate with others and to think. They learn to think symbolically —that is, they learn to think in images inside their heads, and they become able to remember the past and anticipate the future. And they become aware of themselves as persons in relation to other people. The foundation for these essential human skills is laid in your baby's infancy.

This book will help you to understand what your baby's early experiences mean to him and how his growth in infancy contributes to his future development. As you learn about your baby, you can also grow in self-understanding.

The first two years of life are very mysterious to most adults. The experiences you had during that period in your own life are firmly registered in your mind/body memory but are very hard to recall. The two ways you most often use to remember and represent your experiences— words and pictures—weren't available to you when you were a tiny infant, so you can't remember your early experiences in those forms. But those early memories did register.

They are a part of you, and they affect the way you look at and live your life now. In particular, they affect the way you will treat your own baby. How can you get back in touch with those memories so that you can understand yourself better and give your baby the kind of care you want to give her and that she needs?

You have an exciting opportunity. If you are home with your own baby, then you're very fortunate. You have a living laboratory. If you're in a classroom learning about babies, maybe you'll also get a chance to learn with some babies at a day care center, a well-baby clinic, or through babysitting a neighbor's baby. Through your experiences with babies, you can relearn—now on a conscious, aware level—how to experience life as you did when you were a baby. Through learning to take the baby's point of view and putting yourself in her shoes, you will also come to understand some of your own feelings and needs better.

Touch is a baby's first language. It is his primary avenue for learning about the world, and it is through his skin that his first memories are registered. Many adults have forgotten how much they learn with their bodies. They aren't aware of how much their feelings tell them about their world, because they filter those feelings through words and pictures.

If you pay attention to what you communicate to your baby through your touch, as well as what he communicates to you through his response to your handling, his movements, the tension in his body, and so on, you also can learn to understand the language of touch—what it means and how to express it yourself, consciously and deliberately.

For example, when you hold your baby gently and securely while you feed her, she will tell you if she's comfortable by settling calmly into your arms. You communicate feelings of love and security to her, and she communicates her feelings of contentment to you through your skin-to-skin contact.

If your baby spits out the mashed bananas you try to feed her at six weeks and she squirms and frets, she's "telling" you that she's not ready yet to swallow them. At that age, her eating equipment is designed for sucking, and her greatest nutritional need is for milk. Her psychological need is to be held lovingly, skin-to-skin, so she can feel safe and secure.

As your baby gets older, his needs change. This is a sign of growth. In order for your baby to grow fully, his needs at each stage must be satisfied as completely as possible. For example, if you make him feel very safe, secure, and loved when he's very small, then as he learns how to do things for himself, he won't be afraid or hesitant to try out new things.

Too many adults are reluctant or even afraid to try new things, because they never learned to feel really safe and secure; they're comfortable only when things remain the same. You can help your baby, and yourself, too, by helping him satisfy his basic human needs all along the way as he grows.

When your baby learns to do things for herself, she needs practice doing those things. Through doing things for herself, a baby learns to feel good about herself as someone who can have a positive effect on the people and things around her.

Most parents are very enthusiastic about their baby trying out new things such as sitting or walking. But their enthusiasm dims when the new activity is throwing toys on the floor or smearing food on her tray. It's not that such things are so terrible. Certainly they can be annoying, messy, or tiring. But such behavior is usually short-lived. Recognizing what the need is, you often can think of an alternative for your baby to do instead.

For example, when your baby starts trying to take the spoon away from you to feed himself but all he seems to feed is the floor and every part of himself but his mouth, you can compromise by giving him an extra spoon and "taking turns" with him. When he's a little older and starts dumping the contents of wastebaskets, cupboards, and drawers all over the floor, you can make him a "dump and fill" bag of junk mail, buttons, old clothes, and other interesting items.

More often than not, adults get upset when their babies are mischievous because they learned, from the way their parents treated them in their own infancy, that such behaviors are "bad." Most people really don't mean to get angry at their babies for such antics, and it makes them feel bad when it happens. It's just an automatic, learned reaction. It can be unlearned when you understand that your baby doesn't mean any harm with her mischief any more than you did when you were a baby. She's not challenging your authority. She just needs to try out her own skills and influence on the environment. She needs practice in asserting her own needs and interests now in order to be able to do so effectively when she's older and expected to take responsibility.

You can't let a baby do anything he wants. When he wants to do something that could hurt himself or others or that interferes with others' needs, you have to step in and calmly, gently, but firmly stop the action. Distraction and removal from the situation usually works best because babies' memories are short. Sometimes a firm "No!" is necessary. This, however, should be saved for when it's really needed or it loses its effectiveness. Unless your baby is in danger or is hurting someone or something else that can't simply be removed from temptation, he should be allowed as much freedom as possible to explore, experiment, and find out what he can do.

It can take a little time to learn to treat your baby empathically—as if you were in her place—because you may have no practice since your own infancy at looking at the world through a baby's eyes. If you're a first-time parent, unless you've had lots of experience with baby sisters and brothers, you haven't had much practice being a caregiver. But you can learn as you go. And, as long as you're going to learn a new job, why not let your baby help you learn it?

Caring for a baby can be difficult and demanding. And the number of available books intended to help you be a better parent often confuse rather than help. With so many experts telling you what you should do with your children, whom should you trust?

Help Your Baby Learn can help *you* become the expert. Its primary message is that you can trust your own baby to "tell" you what he needs. The book supplies the details you need in order to notice and understand the meanings of the many little things your baby does.

Most books about children are written from an adult point of view. They stress what you should do, and they concentrate almost exclusively on those developmental achievements that make children more adult-like (e.g., talking, walking). Doing this, they often miss many of the more important developmental signals through which growing children tele-graph their needs.

In this book, an involved father and early childhood educator translates the world of the baby into terms adults can understand and act on. Using mini-portraits of his own three babies' experiences to illustrate, Dr. Lehane helps us to understand the meaning of such behaviors as drooling, thumb-sucking, playing with food, and various forms of "mis-chief" from the baby's point of view. Many simple activities are presented through which you can help your baby become increasingly more com-petent and confident by expanding on these signals of learning readiness.

Through *Help Your Baby Learn,* you can become more observant of your baby's day-to-day growth signals. You'll learn what to look for and ways to respond. Knowing what you're doing will give you the confidence to trust your own judgment of what your baby needs in order to grow as happily and fully as possible.

We join with Stephen Lehane in inviting you to "Help Your Baby Learn."

LAURIE D. BRAGA

JOSEPH L. BRAGA

University of Miami
School of Medicine

PREFACE

Help Your Baby Learn describes the day-to-day developments which most babies go through from birth to their second year. It is filled with ideas for activities to do with babies which will help you become more observant and understanding of their behavior while you help them grow.

These activities derive from two sources. First, they are based on the activities we did with our three children, Christopher, Erik, and Erin, to help them develop their bodies, minds, and personalities. These activities, in turn, were based on the developmental theories of Dr. Jean Piaget.*

By providing guidelines for activities to do with your baby, this book can put you in Piaget's shoes, where you can step right into the baby's mind—thereby gaining knowledge and insights that would be unattainable by simply reading about child development.

You will see how important such common, everyday behaviors as sucking, eye-blinking, grabbing, and hide-and-seek are to babies' intellectual growth. Knowing the significance of these otherwise easily overlooked behaviors, you will be better prepared to guide your baby's learning on a day-to-day basis than if you only view as important such conventional landmarks as weaning, crawling, walking, and talking.

Since working out the basics with my children, the activities have been used with parents from many different walks of life, and what worked effectively for us proved to work for others just as well.

---

* Jean Piaget, *The Origins of Intelligence in Children* (New York: W. W. Norton and Co., Inc., 1963).

Through engaging in the suggested activities, you are encouraged to spend more time with your baby—playing with her, changing and growing with her, and constantly trying to understand her world. Hopefully, your experiences will better your understanding of what your baby's behaviors mean—from her point of view. Further, they should teach you where to look when you have questions about what your baby needs: The answers lie in the child.

This is the central message *Help Your Baby Learn* has for all of you who are students of young children, whether you're sitting in a college classroom or at home with a newborn. Closely observing babies during their natural play is an important way to learn about development, and it is available to anyone in contact with children. Further, it is a way that complements the more technical and experimental studies of children.

But this is not just a book to stimulate infant development. As you are helping the baby grow and develop, your experiences will be helping you develop into a wiser and more understanding person.

Look, for example, at our experience with our little girl, Erin, who dissolved into a tantrum when she couldn't pack her valise. My first thought was "How could she take something as silly as this so seriously?" But the key to the answer lay in my question. Obviously, what meant very little to me was very important to Erin. I backed off and tried to look at the situation from Erin's point of view. Then, things began to click. I was able to piece together an explanation based on my knowledge of Erin's misunderstanding of the concept of gravity, i.e., why things fall. Because of this misunderstanding, she couldn't pack her little bag, was overcome with frustration, and broke down.

Here was a clear cut example of a situation in which the baby's intellectual and emotional development criss-crossed with the developing awareness of a parent. If I had not developed and changed, this situation could have been exaggerated into a real emotional crisis.

In situations like the above, or even when your baby does something that really upsets you, such as breaking a valuable antique clock, try to stay calm. Try to remember that the damage done to a prized possession is much easier to repair than the damage done to your baby if you fly off the handle and let your rage go unchecked.

Remaining cool, calm, and understanding is difficult. Having three children, I know this from first hand experience. Also, I know that kids can push you to a breaking point, and I realize how easy it is to lash out; but just remember how cutting your lash could be for a baby. So when you are about to boil over, try to get out of the situation or to have someone relieve you. If neither alternative is possible, then try to put yourself in your baby's place. Surely, he did not intend to hurt or anger you by breaking one of your possessions. It was just an accident.

In fact, most of the mischief babies get into stems from new developments and from the urge to show off these achievements. This is what *Help Your Baby Learn* tries to point out. It shows that behind most of your baby's actions is a developing mind and a well-intentioned personality that's trying to show you, for whom he cares most, what he is all about.

INTRODUCTION

"Make sure Erik does his homework," Mrs. L. reminded her husband. Quite a common remark for parents—unless you know Erik's age. He is not yet a week old.

Erik's parents are using *Help Your Baby Learn*, which contains one hundred activities to help Erik learn and develop during his first two years of life. Today's "homework" is an activity on sucking. Yesterday's dealt with searching for the nipple. And, in the days to come, Erik will be doing activities involving drooling, lip-licking, patty-cake, peek-a-boo, and the like.

Seemingly "unimportant" behaviors have been found by Dr. Jean Piaget to be the landmarks of an infant's intellectual development.[1] *Help Your Baby Learn* takes Piaget's technical findings and puts them into clear-cut language and activities for parents and other infant caregivers. The activities require you to do nothing other than what you're already doing: feeding, changing, and playing with your baby. They simply match your playing with your baby's stage of development, thus helping you help him learn and develop.

But *Help Your Baby Learn* does more; it helps you learn and develop as a parent.

Consider what Mrs. L. had to say about her first-born, Christopher, before she had *Help Your Baby Learn:*

---

[1] Jean Piaget, *The Origins of Intelligence* (New York: W. W. Norton Co., 1963).

1

I fed him, put him to bed, and until he cried I just waited and waited. It seemed endless; a few minutes of wakefulness, hours of sleep, and days of waiting. Chris looked all right, but I began to worry. Am I doing the right things? Shouldn't he do more? I was starved for the slightest sign of change from him. That's why his first smile sent me skyrocketing. I practically jumped into the crib to make him do it again. But no luck. All I got were bubbles and gurgles from his stomach. Slumping back, I again waited for some "big event" to happen, such as smiling, rolling over, sitting up, or crawling. How was I to know that Chris had already been doing and showing me things since day one?

That was Mrs. L. three years ago: She had little confidence and was really in the dark about what Christopher needed. But look at her today with Erik. All the little things that she hadn't noticed before in Christopher, such as drooling, thumb-sucking, blinking the eyes, and the like, she now sees as signs of Erik's intellectual progress. Hardly a day goes by without Mrs. L. either observing some new development in Erik or boosting along his development by matching her play to his needs.

If you think Mrs. L. changed, take a look at her husband, who used to feel funny just feeding a baby, never mind playing with one. In Mr. L.'s words:

But *Help Your Baby Learn* pinned me down and made me look at myself. I was bringing up my kids just as I was brought up, thinking that since my wife was breast feeding, what more could I do? Change diapers? Everything else a baby does seems to come naturally, so I thought. But it's plain to me now that even if he's born with certain behaviors, they can be wasted, like those of a natural athlete, if they are not played up and worked on.

What comes across from the L.'s and from others who've used this book is a new hope, confidence, and belief that they can change themselves and, in turn, play a bigger role in the development of their children. No longer do they see themselves as bystanders merely waiting for the baby to do something. Now they know how and when to act, because they can read the little cues their baby gives off, and because they have a deeper feeling of how their baby sees the world.

This new sense of productivity is catching; and soon the baby picks it up and begins to perform more and more. Out of all this grows a two way relationship—not with the parent as the only giver, but a two-way street, a give and take situation in which both parents and the child give to each other.

Summing up in a national report on early childhood education, a child psychologist, Urie Bronfenbrenner, writes that this kind of a two-way relationship is the key to future learning because it "leads to the development of a strong emotional attachment, which in turn, increases the motivation of the young child to attend to and learn from the mother."[2]

This isn't a revolutionary idea. It's been in the wind for many years, ever since scientists concluded that if babies missed certain experiences, they wouldn't reach their fullest potential. Still, it's not uncommon to hear that all this close attention and extra handling spoils the baby. Nonsense! We think nothing of spending time on the baby's bodily needs, such as feeding and diapering, or of helping him learn to sit up, crawl, or walk. So why all the fuss when we spend time caring for his mind and his feelings? No one expects you to hold your baby all the time. It would drive you crazy. What's being asked is that you remember, while holding him, how much you can do to meet his intellectual and emotional needs.

Like us, babies have needs. But, unlike us, their needs aren't separated from each other; they're all wrapped up together. Yet educational crib toys treat babies as if they had separate needs. Such toys can leave parents with the impression that there's a special place for learning—the crib—and a special place for feeding and changing—your arms. So when the baby has eaten and is powdered and dry, she's whisked off to the bedroom to play with mobiles or jungle gyms—instead of being held.

Dr. Lipsitt, an expert on infant development, has this to say about educational crib toys:

> ı neir stimulation must be in the context of warm, affectionate parentage. The mother who leaves her child alone all day with a mobile and thinks it will make him a brillant child is sadly mistaken. Things must not be substituted for human contact. To be meaningful for children, toys have to be extensions of people. Presently, an expensive or highly sophisticated toy in the absence of attention and affection is a great way of rejecting the child.[3]

Help Your Baby Learn sides with Dr. Lipsitt. All your baby's needs are easily taken care of in one place—your arms. For instance, while a baby is held, he can be fed and played with in a special way: The feeding satisfies his physical needs; the playing stimulates mental growth; and the holding itself will meet his emotional needs.

[2] Urie Bronfenbrenner, "A Report on Longitudinal Evaluations of Preschool Programs, Vol. II: Is Early Intervention Effective?" Dept. of Health, Education, and Welfare, Publication No. (OHS) 74-25, 1974, p. 26.

[3] In Jane Brody, "A Primer for Toddlers: Self-Discovery," *New York Times*, Jan. 16, 1974, p. 62.

What emotions do babies have? First and foremost, they want to be loved. Since they don't have language, we show them love through touch. Over the past few years, the research on holding has been piling up; and it can now be said that "the major effects observed as a consequence of infant stimulation occur in situations where emotional factors are of major importance."[4]

In other words, the emotional make-up of one's early life has a bearing upon the rest of her life. The above quote stirred quite a commotion because of who said it. Usually such words are uttered by professionals whose lives are devoted to the feelings of children. These professionals are often accused of not having cold facts to back their warm sentiments. But this statement was made at the Center for Advanced Study in Developmental Science, Oxford University, by Dr. Seymour Levine. Dr. Levine is a hard-nosed and exact researcher whose experiments generally deal with the central nervous system, brain chemistry, hormonal influences, and the like. And when a distinguished scientist of this leaning speaks on emotions, we generally listen; these are hard facts.

Although there are new people making these findings, the findings themselves are not new. Fifteen years ago, Dr. Mary Ainsworth[5] boiled down these findings into three major points: Hold your baby more; spend more time with him; and gain a detailed knowledge of his development. These three points are the backbone of *Help Your Baby Learn*. Unfortunately, these points can't stand alone—they're just words. Let's face it: parents are no different from anyone else. As Mrs. L. says, "We don't want pep talks. We want the best for our kids, but we're creatures of habit. Unless we see results, words alone aren't going to keep us from slipping back into our old ways."

Many educators have side-stepped this issue. I can still picture one father who went to all the lectures on holding, and who then boasted that he was doing it for three hours a day. He held the baby all right; however, their eyes never met—because his eyes were glued to a TV set. Or I think of the mother who promised to hold her baby an extra ten minutes a day and who spent this time gazing at the clock, waiting for those few minutes to tick away.

---

[4] Seymour Levine, "Infant Stimulation, A Perspective," in *Stimulation in Early Infancy*, ed. Anthony Ambrose (New York: Academic Press, 1969), p. 5.

[5] Mary Ainsworth, "The Development of Infant-Mother Interactions among the Ganda," in *Determinants of Infant Behavior II*, ed. B. M. Foss (London: Methuen and Co., 1963), 67-112.

Parents will do more than just go through the motions if they are given specific things to do and if there's a payoff. The payoff in *Help Your Baby Learn* is being able to see your baby learn and develop on a daily basis. For example, ordinary things that went unnoticed before, such as lip-licking, will never slip by once you learn that a little act like this signals a giant step in your baby's intellectual development. What lip-licking signifies is that he's breaking away from his reflexes and beginning to think for himself.

Behaviors you thought of as simply being messy, such as drooling, thumb-sucking, and throwing food, will now be looked at in a different light. Take the last case, throwing food. It shows that your baby, in much the same way as physicists do, is trying to figure out the flight path or trajectory of objects as she considers various angles, distances, and weights of the projectile.

"Come off it," laughed Mrs. L., "Christopher threw food just to bother me." She's partly right; for it's not only the mind that changes, but the personality as well. About the time Christopher is able to handle such concepts as trajectory, his personality is moving into the stage of playing games; and you're usually the target of his teasing and fooling.

Piaget doesn't discuss personality in detail; but psychoanalyst Erik Erikson does.[6] He feels that, during the first year, babies need to form a close and trusting tie with the parent, and then that, during the second year, they need to tear loose from the parent and become more independent or autonomous.

From studying babies, both my own and those in various research projects, I've found that sandwiched in between trust and autonomy are several other personality stages that go along with each stage of the baby's intellectual development.

Like Piaget, I have found that all infants go through the same stages of intellectual development. Some go through these stages fast, others move more slowly; some skip behaviors; and a few may tack on some new steps, while others take detours. But, by the time they're two years old, most babies will have passed through the following six stages. Rather than using Piaget's technical terms for these stages, I've chosen ones that I think are clearer; and I have also added on my views about personality development.

[6]Erik Erikson, *Childhood and Society*, 2nd ed. (New York: W. W. Norton Co., 1963).

Intellectual		Personality
Stage 1	Unwinding (0-2 months)	Trusting
Stage 2	Self Discovery (1-6 months)	Showing Off
Stage 3	Finding His Surroundings (4-10 months)	Cocky
Stage 4	Developing Tools (8-14 months)	Buckling Down
Stage 5	Experimenting (12-20 months)	Fun and Games
Stage 6	Winding Up (18-24 months)	Turning Inward

As you can see, the personality and intellect are tied together. This is well described by Professor White's theory of *competency motivation.*[7] Simply stated, the theory says that human beings are moved to act by a need to increase their mastery of themselves and their environment. People's abilities are hooked up to their emotions: The more a person can do, the better she feels about herself—which leads to a sense of competence. To keep this feeling of competence alive, a person must keep changing and growing.

For the baby, this means he has a big job ahead of him. In two years he has to grow, develop, learn, and work out a personality, just as you have to work at being a parent. Neither job comes easily, especially ours—since we have to change first. As I said earlier, the baby picks up or imitates our changes, actions, feelings, and moods. If you do a lot for him, he in turn does a lot for you. If this productivity fills you with pride and confidence, then your baby takes on these same feelings about himself. He will do as you do—not as you say. This is where *Help Your Baby Learn* comes in. It tells you not merely why to change but how to change.

It starts at birth.
It explains the thinking behind your baby's everyday behavior.
It has one hundred activities to help this thinking along.
It supplies guides, in case your baby can't do an activity.
And it has a diary.

In the diary, somewhere near the beginning, Mrs. L. writes, "Who would believe Erik could do so much. I don't have to wait 'til he's older. His growth starts on day one and so does the part I play in it."

[7] Robert White, "Competence and Psychosexual Stages of Development," in *Nebraska Symposium on Motivation,* ed. Marshall R. Jones (Lincoln, Nebr.: University of Nebraska Press, 1960), 7-140.

HOW TO USE
HELP YOUR
BABY LEARN

ACTIVITIES

1. Each chapter in the book deals with a certain age/stage. Find the chapter that covers your baby's age.

2. Start with the first activity in the chapter. If your baby can't do that activity, try some from the preceding chapter until you find her level.

3. When your baby finishes, move on to the second, third, and so on. This is the plan of the book—to do the activities in order.

4. For some activities, your baby will need more time, and for others, less time. He'll also do things not found in this book. This shows that he, like each baby, is unique and learns in special ways. Whenever his special needs come up, you'll have to ignore the book's plan and skip around for activities to fit his needs.

5. If you skip ahead, make sure you read the earlier activities so that the one you're working on makes sense.

6. Always check the guides when your baby can't do an activity or when you think it's time to move on.

7. Try holding your baby during the activities.

8. After each activity, whenever possible, reference is made to another activity in a future stage. This gives you an idea of how your baby's present behavior is related to her future development. Your baby will not be ready for this advanced work until most of the activities in her present stage are completed.

GUIDES

If your baby can't do an activity, try the following:

1. *Try a different toy.* Your baby may be bored by the activity; so try using a different toy, such as a ball, comb, brush, or the like. Make sure these, like all toys, are safe and clean.

2. *Rehearse* or "walk" your baby through the activity. For example, if the activity requires him to grab a toy, put it into his hands and fold his fingers over the toy.

3. You do the activity, and see if she can copy it. As babies develop, they become more capable of *imitation.*

4. Some babies really respond to a *challenge.* If he is supposed to drop toy *A* and pick up *B*, you may have to shake toy *B*, stroke his hand with it, or dangle it in front of his eyes in order to help him pick up toy *B*.

5. Sometimes she merely has to *practice* the activity for a time before she gets the hang of it. When she has had enough, she will stop herself.

6. The last point leads to *timing*, which is the most important guide. This simply means that you shouldn't rush or push your baby through an activity. Occasionally, a baby can't seem to perform a behavior that he could do at an earlier stage. This indicates that the earlier behavior happened by chance or accident. If your baby can do the activity a number of times, without fumbling or hesitating, this is a good sign that he has mastered it. Only when he can perform on such a regular basis, and at will, is the behavior considered fully developed. This ability to act on a regular basis, and not by accident, is a good rule to help you keep your sense of timing. If you don't have this sense of timing and if you rush him through activities, you will have missed one of the main purposes of *Help Your Baby Learn:* developing a sensitivity to your baby's subtle cues, so that you can better "read" and understand his needs.

7. Throughout all the activities and guides, *talk to her* about what she's doing.

8. If your baby cries or gets frustrated during an activity, then stop. The next time you use the activities, go to the one that he's mastered—the one that is easy for him—then start working from there.

These are the general guides. After each activity, you will find one or two guides to specific things you can do with your baby. If the specific guides don't work, it's a good practice to come back and review the general guides for more ideas.

DIARY

After each activity, you'll find a special place for keeping notes about your baby.

Some parents fill the diary with personal thoughts and feelings as they watch their baby, day by day, grow and develop.

Others combine their feelings with a record, describing such things as: (1) how their baby did the activity, (2) when she did it, (3) how long it took from start to finish, (4) whom she did it with, and (5) how the guides worked.

Regardless of how you do it, a baby diary is priceless. Think of what a lock of hair, baby shoes, and old photos do for you. Now imagine your child's feelings when he grows and reads the story of his life as it started from day one.

UNWINDING

Birth to Two Months

Your baby is ready to learn at birth. Although he has spent the last nine months in rather cramped quarters, this has not cramped his development. He is born with reflexes, the building blocks of intelligence. He merely needs to unwind and stretch out after his cramped journey, and then these reflexes will be ready to use.

Like all early behaviors, the reflexes at first are rough and clumsy. However, they quickly grow more refined, and soon the baby does things that she could never do before. Every time your baby does something new, it's a signal that her mind is developing.

One thing to remember about newborns is that they're making progress every day. But their progress is hardly noticeable unless you know what to look for. For instance, sucking—a common behavior normally associated only with eating—is really linked to your baby's mental development. Let's zero in on it for a moment to see just how sucking reflects this development.

At birth, your baby needs the whole nipple in her mouth before she can tell whether or not to suck it. Within a fairly short period of time, she will suck merely when the outside, or dry part, of the lips is touched. This means that she's learning to discriminate; that is, she's developing the ability to distinguish between different experiences.

The next thing sucking signals is a change in the way your baby figures out problems dealing with heights and distances. Have you ever seen your baby stab himself on his chin or nose with the nipple? Usually, this means that the nipple was too high or too low—that is, it was touching only the upper or lower lip. Without making the proper adjustments, the baby lunges forward, ending up with the nipple pressed against his nose or chin. When this happens, he's puzzled; however, in a few moments he makes the needed adjustments simply by moving his head up or down, and he sucks the nipple.

After a couple of experiences like this your baby gets the idea. As soon as one of his lips is touched, he flips his head into position, and sucks the nipple.

Each of these little sucking episodes signals developments being made by your baby's mind. It's a mind on the move, progressing from reflexes to discrimination to problem solving—all within the first few days of life.

Sucking isn't the only behavior giving off signals. Others, such as searching, smiling, thumb-sucking, seeing, hearing, grabbing, and holding are also sending out signals. You can't pick only one behavior to look at; they must all be considered. In fact, some of the behaviors just mentioned go right on developing and giving off signals through the next stage.

Learning and development would go along much faster if your baby could move around and find things herself. But she's still too immature. Everything she needs—food, warmth, touch, stimulation—your baby must get from you. She entrusts her life to you.

The way you handle this trust—how you meet her needs, knowing when and how to act—provides the background for the development of your baby's personality. The development of the branch of her personality which concerns her capacity to open up, love, and take in people rests on the strength of this early trust.

Having a good relationship with your baby, and being tuned into his signals, are important steps in making sure the trust starts off firm and strong. Unfortunately, not all parents have this kind of relationship with their babies.

Some *press.* That is, the mother and father push the baby to do what they want. Others *fall back.* They sense the baby needs something. But they don't have confidence in their ability to figure out and satisfy his needs. So, they just stop what they're doing, believing that "the baby knows best, so let him alone."

However, some grownups really have a good relationship with their babies; they can *shift* or match their needs to the baby's.

Let's hear from some of these different parents.

Judy B. (Pressing): "If she wets in the middle of nursing, I change her, even though she frets and cries."

Pat W. (Shifting): "I'll let Carol finish her bottle and doze off before I change her. It doesn't bother her then. She usually sleeps through it."

Buddy G. (Pressing): "Look—I've got to get Stevie to the sitter by eight. I can't wait until he's finished rolling and squirming. He has to be dressed now."

George M. (Shifting): "Most of the time I'm in a rush when I have to dress her. To make it easier for both of us, I tickle and squeeze Mary and pump her legs up and down. In no time she's dressed."

Betty B. (Falling Back): "I can tell when Chucky is going to cry. He frowns and wrinkles the bags under his eyes. I just let him cry it out and then go back to him."

The best signal Chucky has for showing he's in need is crying. If, like Betty B., you seldom respond—if the best he has doesn't work— then there's a good chance that he'll start feeling powerless, weak, incompetent, ignored, and forgotten. . . all the things that can add up to a cold, mistrustful, and closed personality. Fortunately, a personality that's started in infancy isn't something you're stuck with forever. There's always time to change, but it does get harder with age. The reason for this is that, according to Dr. Arnold Gesell, "the rate of growth during the first week of life, could we measure it, far exceeds that of any comparable interval of growth in later infancy."[1] Maybe the first week is just as crucial for parents. So try shifting now.

The key to shifting is to keep up with your baby's changing signals. In addition to those already mentioned, there are some others worth noting—signals that deal chiefly with your baby's physical development.

What comes across as soon as you handle your baby is how weak and loose her muscles are: She can't lift her head without support, and her eyes simply float around without focusing. There's also a breakdown in coordination: Her lips and tongue don't work well together, thus making it hard to swallow solid foods. In fact, she may gag if fed solids before the third or fourth month. With time, these limitations disappear as the muscles grow stronger and tighter.

In summary, your baby starts the unwinding stage with built-in reflexes and then refines them into well-developed behaviors for discriminating and problem-solving.

[1] Arnold Gesell, *The Mental Growth of the Pre-school Child* (New York: The Macmillan Co., 1925).

Now that you have some idea of what's going on during this stage, turn to the activities and try them out as you play with your baby.

1. NIBBLERS, TESTERS, AND CHOKERS

From birth, we could see differences in our children. Christopher was a nibbler; Erin a tester; and Erik a choker—so named because he would nearly gag on or try to swallow the entire nipple before he would ever start sucking.

Our babies were showing us three forms of discrimination. Chokers don't discriminate well; they need to swallow virtually the entire nipple before they know enough to act. Nibblers like Christopher can discriminate easily; they can recognize the slightest touch on the lips as a signal to start sucking. Erin is in the middle; she needs a few moments of testing the nipple with her tongue before her sucking is triggered.

The move from choker to tester to nibbler doesn't take very long. Indeed, this change represents one of the earliest signs that your baby is making intellectural process. Now he can *discriminate*. Without this ability, his mental development would come to a standstill.

Discrimination also contributes to the baby's emotional make-up. For example, how could the baby establish trust if he couldn't distinguish or discriminate between people who were kind, helpful, and nurturing and those who were not? Without this ability, survival alone would require an infant to be mistrustful, suspicious, and withdrawn— hardly the characteristics you would want your child to acquire.

Let's see how well your baby is progressing. While holding him, brush his lips. Does he suck? Or does the nipple have to be thrust deep into his mouth before he begins to suck? Is he startled by the nipple going so deep? Will he suck if you brush his lips with your finger? Or do you have to put it in his mouth?

The purpose of this activity is to observe your baby's power to discriminate. Progress in this skill can be seen in Activity 13.

DIARY

_____

_____

_____

_____

_____

GUIDE

If brushing the lips does not set off sucking, then try the tongue or gums.

For many babies, sucking depends on the place where they're stimulated: lips, tongue, or mouth. For others, it's the object: nipple, finger, or rattle. Finally, there are some babies whose sucking is touched off by a combination of touching a certain place with a certain object.

Try these different combinations. They all reflect your baby's growing powers of discrimination.

2. THE FUSSY EATER

Erin was one of the fussiest eaters I ever saw. After sucking anything, she would always pause to express her tastes with arching brows, bulging eyes, or cold stares. At times you would swear she was right on the verge of saying, "I can't stomach this!" or "What did you put in my mouth?"

All babies have such feelings, especially in relation to different tastes and temperatures.

Your baby's reaction to sweetness and sourness, as well as to hot and cold, is the next development we are going to examine. It's based on a new form of discrimination that's much more sensitive than the various forms of sucking.

Dip the corner of a clean washcloth into some sugar water and let your baby suck it. What happens? What is her reaction? Now try it with a little salt water. Record how she reacts.

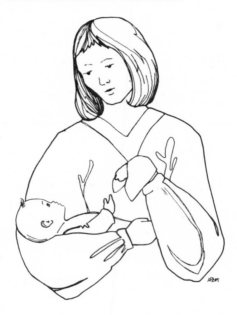

The impact these two tastes have on a baby depends on her personality. If she's high-strung, you can expect wild arm-waving, head-twisting, and, perhaps, wrenched and sealed lips. A low-keyed baby might only pat her arms, shift her head, and pucker her lips. Unlike the high-strung baby with her outbursts, the low-keyed infant keeps things inside and is harder to read. Although you could easily ignore or dominate these babies, such actions would cut off their development of trust. Your baby's reaction to different tastes signals not only an intellectual development, but one of personality as well.

You can gain additional information about your baby's mind and personality by observing her reactions to temperature changes.

Soak the wash cloth in some lukewarm water. Put a corner in her mouth and watch her action. Next try ice water. How does she show her feelings? Are they like the ones that surfaced when she sucked the sweet and salty water?

During this play your baby is demonstrating how refined her discrimination has become just within the first few days of life. This refinement and precision become extraordinary during Activity 14.

DIARY

_____

_____

_____

_____

_____

_____

_____

_____

_____

GUIDE

If your baby can easily distinguish between various tastes and temperatures, then see if she can discriminate among various sizes, shapes, and textures. What's her reaction when sucking a straw, a wash cloth, a metal spoon, a plastic rattle, a rubber ball, a wooden block?

3. IN A HURRY TO EAT

Christopher could never wait to eat; he was always in a rush. Often this led to his being stabbed in the chin or on the nose with a nipple, instead of its landing in his mouth. Guiding the mouth to the nipple requires a sophisticated understanding of spatial concepts such as above and below, close and far.

Increasingly, as the baby works out his understanding, it becomes clear that he can get whatever he desires only if it's close by. Things far away are no help to him. This applies to you as well as to toys, blankets, milk bottles, and the like. In fact, he begins to attach certain feelings to specific parts of space: a sense of emptiness to the concept of distance and a sense of well-being to the concept of closeness. In other words, he feels good when you're close and uncertain when you're away. Here's another point where the mind and personality interact with other.

To get an idea of your baby's early *concept of space*, tilt the nipple so it only grazes his upper lip. What happens? Does he take the initiative and lunge forward? If so, the nipple probably stabbed him on the nose. Does he make any adjustments? Does he raise his head to the proper height so that he can suck the nipple? How many tries before he realizes that he must change his position in order to get closer?

Here the baby is learning about space. He continues to do this throughout his first two years of life. For example, in Activity 23 you'll have an opportunity to observe your baby learning that his face is made up of different spaces: an upper part with eyes, a lower part with a mouth, and a middle with a nose.

DIARY

_____

_____

_____

_____

_____

GUIDE

It is easier for some babies to learn to drop their heads to suck than to learn to raise their heads. If this seems to be true for your baby, see what happens if you brush his lower lip with a rattle.

4. WILD SEARCHING

Imagine a bee snarled and buzzing in your hair. Just picture how frantically you would shake and twist your head, impulsively searching for a way to dislodge the insect. Well, this was Erik whenever he nestled into our arms.

What ignites this frenzied head-turning is the _searching reflex:_ a built-in drive for acquiring food that is triggered when the cheeks are touched.
could interpret this as a rejection of food, or even as a rejection of

This wild head-swinging looks as if the baby is desperately saying "No, No, No!" An anxious couple having trouble feeding their baby themselves as adequate parents. In reality this is just a hungry baby whose reflex causes her to hunt frantically for food. Relax. Don't pull the nipple away or try to soothe your baby. Simply be patient and work with her, while trying to guide the nipple into her mouth.

Before long, there's progress. Now, when she is touched, the baby turns only in one direction—towards the cheek that was stimulated.

From here on in, her mind is capable of decoding signals: A touch on the right cheek means a right turn, while a touch on the left cheek results in a turn to the left. Earlier, she had relied solely on the searching reflex, a mechanism capable of picking up incoming signals but totally incapable of sending out the specific behaviors appropriate to the signals received.

In a short time, your baby has made record progress. Spatial concepts involving up and down and horizontal movements are well understood. And now she's on the verge of mastering left and right turns—an achievement indicating that your baby is close to understanding the concept of laterality, which will eventually help her to acquire different notions about space and direction.

Some babies search in all directions when their cheek is slightly touched, but only in one direction when it's rubbed. Try both. Does your baby respond differently to these differing pressures? Does she just sweep her head back and forth or does she swing it madly? Do her lips suck?

As you play with the baby in this way, you'll see her trying to regulate her reflexes so that they're less impulsive and more controlled. This is one of the primary functions of the "Unwinding Stage."

DIARY

_____

_____

_____

_____

_____

GUIDE

The best time to try this is just before the baby finishes eating, when she's still alert and sensitive to incoming signals.

5. CALM SEARCHING

Christopher was getting very cagey—just like a hunter. Rather than snaring anything that touched his cheek, he waited, as if baiting a trap. Now, unless he was brushed near his mouth, he did little searching or hunting.

At this point, his mind can work out reasonable expectations. He figures that food and other interesting things usually travel close to the mouth, while those things touching the brow, chin, jaw, and even parts of the cheek seldom signal anything really interesting or tasty.

Backing up this reasoning is a feeling of trust that you are not out to trick or tease him. He knows you won't play around with anything important but will bring it straight to his mouth so that he may either eat or study it.

Using your finger, brush under your baby's eye and slowly move down towards his mouth. At what point does searching begin? Does he look startled or show any reactions as you brush his jaw, chin, or nose?

From this play it seems that the searching reflex has changed from a blind and undirected action to one that's being calmly directed and monitored. You can experience a dramatic change in the grasping reflex when you work with Activity 28.

DIARY

_____

_____

_____

_____

_____

GUIDE

If your baby searches no matter where you brush him, it may be that your finger reminds him of the nipple. To test this, try brushing him with a washcloth or with something that gives him a feeling other than that of flesh.

6. SUCKING THE WRIST

While waiting to eat, Erin would usually suck her wrist; she no longer sucked her blanket: She was getting choosey. At this point in her development, your baby's cheeks can distinguish the touches of a hand, shirt, and nipple from that of the satin trim on a blanket. Remarkably, this trim, although it feels very much like your skin, won't set off searching. Your baby has learned that satin merely leads to a wooly blanket, but that your skin or shirt usually signals the coming of food, warmth, security, or stimulation.

Your baby's ability to distinguish among similar things, such as satin trim, your skin, or a rubber toy, has grown since birth. Such sharp powers of discrimination will be called on later as she works with various concepts and symbols. They are important now in her learning to deal with different people. Some infants are so used to being handled in certain ways, that can discriminate among different individuals on the basis of touch. Does your baby show any preferences or different responses to being touched by mom, dad, or the kids?

What's interesting is that the roots of discrimination, like other important intellectual and emotional developments, start with early searching and seeking—behaviors normally associated merely with eating.

To see what makes your baby search, touch her cheek, in turn, with your finger, a sweater, a washcloth, a rattle and a rubber ball. Which ones have the least effect on her? Which ones really cause searching? Does her searching differ with different materials?

This activity was designed to see if your baby could *accommodate*, or alter her behaviors to fit the object she's playing with. Although still primitive, this accommodation does make some progress, as you will see, when you do Activity 19.

DIARY

_____

_____

_____

_____

_____

_____

_____

_____

GUIDE

To determine how powerful your baby's discrimination is, simultaneously touch each of her cheeks with a different object—your finger and a rattle. What reactions do you observe? Is she confused? Does she prefer the finger and turn to that side? Does she turn to one side and then switch to the other?

7. THUMB-SUCKING

At birth, all babies try to suck their thumbs. We have even seen pictures of fetuses, floating in their amniotic sacs, doing it. Such experiences give you the impression that thumb-sucking is natural: something all babies can do at birth. However, the truth of the matter is that sucking is not inborn; it's learned.

To be sure, it can be done occasionally, but not on a regular basis. Such occasional sucks are merely accidental, produced only after many trials and errors. The baby can't place his thumb in his mouth whenever he wishes. It takes weeks before his mind has developed the necessary hand to mouth coordination.

You can see just how uncoordinated your baby is by holding him out in front of you. Such a position seems to set off an alarm for thumb-sucking. Although he tries to suck, he ends up madly flapping his arms in the air while he shakes his head aimlessly from side to side.

The first signs of coordination surface when the baby is snugly cradled in your arms. He uses your shirt as a guide, rubbing against it with his hands and mouth until they meet, and then he jams his thumb into his mouth. Once thumb-sucking starts, he stiffens his whole body and directs his full concentration to keeping his thumb in place.

Remember, the chief way your baby learns during this stage is by sticking things in his mouth. Until now, you've been bringing things to his mouth. From here on, starting with thumb-sucking, he's beginning to do this for himself. It's the first step in becoming an autonomous learner, if not an autonomous person.

Unfortunately, some parents see thumb-sucking only as a dirty, sloppy habit, one to be discouraged. Thus, this new behavior may usher in the first struggle between your needs and those of the baby. Try to see your baby's thumb-sucking from his point of view, because pressing or pushing your will on him will interfere with your building a relationship of trust.

Let's see how well your baby's hand to mouth coordination has progressed while you're cuddling him. Can he suck his thumb? Notice his hands and mouth; does he move both towards each other? If he keeps one stationary or moves it erratically, this indicates that his coordination is undeveloped.

The purpose of this activity is to determine the extent of your baby's *hand to mouth coordination.* By the time you're working with Activity 16 you'll have further opportunity to gauge the development of this coordination.

DIARY

_____

_____

_____

_____

GUIDE

Sometimes the cuddling doesn't work because it's too enclosing. Your baby may need more room to warm up his arms before moving them towards his mouth. Try laying him on his stomach. Does this position make thumb-sucking easier?

We'll return to thumb-sucking in the next stage, at which time it reaches full development.

8. SMILING

Erik was a delightful baby. After each nap he would wake up with a smile.

Smiling is one behavior we all look forward to but don't always understand. To many it is a sign of affection: The baby is returning our love. But this isn't always the case, especially during the first few weeks of life, when smiling can be brought on by such things as the sound of a high-pitched voice, a bright light, tickling, and other kinds of touching.

Like thumb-sucking, real social smiling isn't just an automatic behavior. It takes time to develop and it hinges on two cognitive activities: the capacity to discriminate between likes and dislikes and the ability to coordinate the senses. If your baby sees something and judges it nice or pleasant, this message is conveyed to her mouth, which then smiles.

Smiling is an intellectual activity before it becomes one denoting affection. Unless you realize this, it's possible to become depressed, feeling, perhaps, that your baby isn't smiling because you haven't given her enough love.

Since smiling entails such complex intellectual operations, it often requires—at least during these early days—large dosages of stimuli before it comes into play. To evoke smiling, try the following: Simultaneously move around, sing, and rock the baby. Does she smile? Next, use only one activity. What happens? Out of three, is there one activity that works best for getting her to smile?

As you can see, the aim of this activity is to determine what stimuli evoke smiling in your baby. During Activity 17 you'll be able to assess how much more sensitive and responsive your baby has become to various stimuli.

DIARY

_____

_____

_____

_____

_____

_____

_____

_____

GUIDE

Some babies smile more for toys than for people. Show your baby a rubber duck: Shake it, make it produce noise, and rub it on her cheek. Does she smile more for the toy than for just you?

In the next stage we will re-examine smiling to see how much it has progressed.

9. VISION

I was never certain how well newborns like Christopher could see. Curious to find out, I would dive-bomb him constantly plastering my big burly face in front of his tiny eyes, startling the wits out of him.

Those days are behind. Babies can't see quite as well as we do, but they do see pretty well. Just switch on a lamp and watch your baby

turn from whatever he's doing to glare at the light. Babies have other visual preferences in addition to bright lights: your face, blinking lights, richly colored toys, moving objects, and complex drawings—somewhat like abstract patterns on some wall paper.

Eventually as his eyes strengthen and develop, your baby will no longer bring objects solely to his mouth for exploration. He also will deliver them to his eyes for study and examination, much in the same way adults do when studying and learning. But, even before he reaches this level of development, your baby is capable of doing a lot of learning with his eyes.

Point a small light toward your baby's face. Does he look straight at it? Move the light closer, then back off. Does his expression change with the movement? Shake your finger. Can he follow it? Swing your finger 180° from shoulder to shoulder. Does he track it? Does he turn his head or eyes?

As the baby practices his focusing and tracking, keep in mind that shortly his eyes will be playing a much bigger part in his learning and development. See Activity 26.

DIARY

GUIDE

If your baby doesn't follow your finger, try swinging a brightly colored toy in front of his eyes.

Currently, his eyes sometimes seem just to wander. Within a few weeks, there'll be marked improvement in concentrating and focusing as he enters the next stage of development.

10. HEARING

In contrast to my testing of Christopher's vision, I had no doubts that he could hear. The mere fact that I tip-toed through the house during nap time was enough evidence of this. Actually, most ordinary noises won't disturb a baby's sleep, but psychologists believe that very loud noises can trigger an inborn fear in the baby.

Perhaps our concern over waking the baby or causing her fright is so overwhelming that we have not noticed the effects of other sounds upon her. For example, soft sounds, such as muffled voices, padded footsteps, and squeaking furniture, tend to arouse a state of curiosity in your baby. Watch what happens when such a noise reaches your baby while she is sucking. The eyes shift, sucking slows up, and she pauses briefly before resuming sucking.

Now consider the suspicion arousal caused by a strange noise. Notice her eyes darting wildly, her sucking coming to a full halt, her face becoming strained and drawn and then slowly letting loose as sucking starts again very cautiously.

The shifting or darting eyes indicate that your baby is now in the process of making simple coordinations between what she sees and what she hears. Like all coordinations, this reflects a growing mental maturity.

Try the following activities with your baby: While she is sucking the nipple, make some noises. Cough, sing, whistle, talk, whisper, tap your feet, snap your fingers, and so on.

Does she stop sucking? Do some sounds have more effect on her than others? Which ones?

Hearing is pretty well developed at this point. In the next stage, the baby will be able to coordinate her hearing and sight, as is demonstrated in Activity 20.

DIARY

_____

_____

_____

_____

_____

GUIDE

If the baby doesn't pay much attention to your noises, try toy noises: Squeeze her duck, wind the music box, shake a rattle, ring a bell, and so on.

11. INDEPENDENCE

Up to this point, Erin was totally dependent on us for food as well as for intellectual nourishment. If toys were not supplied, there would be little learning.[1] Fortunately this soon changes with the emergence of *prehension* as shown by the ability to grab toys and bring them to oneself for study and examination.

As important as this is to intellectual progress, it may be even more important to the baby's personality development. No longer totally reliant on you, she now starts growing more independent. Although sparked by prehensible ability, this independence would never have surfaced unless she was secure and stable. Having such a bond of trust—a feeling of confidence and security with you—the baby now goes out on her own to discover and learn through prehension.

If the newborn baby's palm is touched by a finger, it is grabbed, and then immediately released; only during nursing will the finger be held, and then merely for a few seconds. Within a short time, there's a dramatic change. Now when her palm is touched, your baby will grab your finger and completely stop searching. Soon, the drive for prehension is so strong that it can distract the baby from sucking. This indicates a fantastic shift of interest to the hands, an interest capable of overtaking the baby's chief preoccupation—eating. Watch this interest soar over the next couple of weeks as your baby repeatedly practices this grabbing: slowly opening, closing, and bending the fingers.

---

[1] Of course, even more important than toys is the company of other human beings.

The more experiences your baby has with different objects, the more skillful her grasping becomes. Try touching her palms with smooth and with rough scraps of cloth, or with wood and plastic toys. Do you get different reactions? Which one does she grab firmly? Does she grab all of them? If you move away from the center and only touch the edge of her palm, does she still grab?

With this play you can see that your baby is trying to make some contact with the outside world by grabbing anything that touches her palm. In the next stage, through Activities 23 to 28, you'll record how much progress you baby has made in trying to grasp and understand the world around her.

DIARY

_____

_____

_____

_____

_____

_____

_____

GUIDE

If grabbing different objects seems easy, then see if your baby will practice her prehension without toys. Moisten her palm with warm and then with cold water. Does this cause her to open and close her hand? Does she continue to play with her hands? Does she now focus interest on her hands? Does this lead to her practicing grasping in the absence of a toy or prop?

12. CRYING: A CHAIN REACTION

With nose pressed hard against the nursery window, trying to get a glimpse of Erik, I can still remember thinking, "Why does the hospital separate us with such thick glass?" At that moment a doctor opened the door to the nursery and I had my answer loud and clear as the blast from thirty screaming babies almost caused my ears to cave in.

Actually, all this yelling is a sign of early intellectual development known as *learning by contagion.* Once a baby starts screaming, the others interpret his crying as their own, so it is picked up by all and kept going like a chain reaction. This is a good reason why it would be better for newborns to be with their mothers rather than housed all together.

Contagion learning can really become frustrating at home if you or your neighbors have other children, for when they cry, your baby will start. To muffle the cries from neighboring babies, parents may lull their child to sleep with music from a record player or by singing to him.

Although such learning lingers on for the next few months, it will eventually be displaced by other developments such as *mutual imitation:* You imitate the baby, and then he imitates you.

As your baby sticks out his tongue, you do the same. What are his reactions? Does he copy you? Sometimes you will have to wave your tongue from side to side before he follows. Is this the case with your baby? Does his facial expression show that he realizes you are copying each other?

This play reveals that your baby can imitate on a very basic level. Imitation is an ability that develops slowly over at least a year's time. However, during each stage some progress is evident, as you'll experience in Activity 22.

DIARY

_____

_____

_____

_____

_____

_____

_____

GUIDE

Try making a sucking noise; can your baby copy this? Do you notice your baby copy any of your other routine behavior?

stage two   **SELF-DISCOVERY**

One to Six Months

About this time your baby seems to settle into a routine. She's no longer a novelty. What she eats, how long she sleeps, when she wets, and so on are pretty well nailed down. So now some of your considerations swing to the rest of the family, to housework, friends, school, or to your job.

Then suddenly, without warning, the calm is ripped with an explosion of activities from your baby. Gushing from everywhere are things you've never seen. Where sounds never bothered her before, now she'll freeze like a hunting dog at the slightest squeak or the softest voice. A moving shadow, a dim change of light, or a little doll is enough to strain and bulge her eyes. What was once a stone face is now all rubbery and full of smiles, laughs, and giggles. And nothing gets by her. Her mind has a tremendous outreach. It's like wildfire, gobbling and lapping up whatever it sees, hears, or touches. Nothing's safe: Buttons, thumbs, fingers, towels, and rattles are all grabbed and sucked.

What's happened? She's discovered herself and all the things she can do. Throughout the "Unwinding Stage", your baby was stretching her bumpy reflexes into smooth and controlled behaviors. Now she's learning how to coordinate or tie together a number of these behaviors. For example, she can pick up rattles, move them to her mouth, and suck them. This type of behavior marks the second stage of infant

35

development, called "Self-discovery."In this time period, your baby begins to find out what she can do.

You can see signs of this newly formed control by watching your baby lick his lips. Notice how relaxed and wide awake he is and how his arms move rhythmically. Earlier, this licking would have jolted him into wild arm-waving and furious sucking, because during "Unwinding," the slightest touch on the lips, such as licking, was an automatic signal or reflex to start sucking for food. Things are different in "Self-discovery." Touching the lips does not always mean food. Now, from your baby's point of view, it means, "I am playing and just practicing to control my tongue."

This licking is a great leap forward. Before, your baby had to spring into action, like a trap, whenever her reflexes were touched. But now she is her own boss; she has more control over herself.

If you want to see how "expert" she is becoming in body control, watch her as she rolls saliva over her lips. Earlier, she would drool all over her chin. But now, when saliva dangles like a yo-yo from your baby's chin, she can, in the nick of time, snap it up and swallow it before it has time to fall.

If this looks like showing off, it is. In order to keep you close by, and to stop your attention from swinging to others, your baby starts showing off and becomes more outgoing. Here is a clear example of how the mind and personality work together: The baby in this stage has a mind and a personality that reach out.

This personality stems from the earlier experiences your baby has had with you. The trust, warmth, and respect you exhibited during the "Unwinding Stage" have now rubbed off so that your baby feels confident, secure, and powerful enough to try to control things on his own. As with any new-found power, it often comes on too strong, hence the appearance of showing off.

Although *Help Your Baby Learn* takes a look at personality, it doesn't cover the entire waterfront. It picks out those parts of the baby's personality which not only affect the parent but which the parent can also affect. This gets back to the importance of the two-way relationship. In this case you swing away; and then your baby shows off, so you swing back. Dr. Brazelton, a pediatrician at Harvard Medical School, has studied this showing off or attention-getting in infants. It seems to happen a lot during this stage, as when the baby plays alone for ten or fifteen minutes and then shows off, cries, or flirts with you by smiling in order to get you to come over and stay a while.

Although we're pushovers for a smile, many of us have the opposite reaction to thumb-sucking, another behavior that shows up along with smiling during "Self-discovery." Occasionally things can get rough between you and your baby if you view thumb-sucking as something to be discouraged instead of seeing it as a sign of intellectual progress.

No matter how you view thumb-sucking, this is still going to be a bumpy period. We have to learn to shift our behavior to meet the new needs our baby has as he jumps ahead into new developments. Changes in physical make-up alone are hard enough to deal with. Those slippery ones involving the mind and personality are even harder. Take the neck, for instance: Its muscles are so strong that if your baby is propped up or held, she can sit for a long time. In fact she prefers this position and yells if she is kept on her back. It's easy to misread the yelling as a sign that your baby is tired, when it really means that she wants to sit up so that more and better contact can be made with you. Check your baby's eyes when she is sitting up: Earlier, they were uncoordinated, aimlessly dancing around; now, like arrows, her eyes can zoom right in on the tiniest objects. Five, ten, or fifteen minutes is nothing for her eyes to spend studying her hands as they play around with everything in sight. This is time well spent, for it leads to eye–hand coordination and eventually to prehension.

Speaking of time, your baby's body is now on an entirely new schedule. Before, he woke, ate, and slept; now he wakes, plays, eats, plays some more, and then sleeps. If you're out of step with this schedule, you might end up forcing him to nap when he doesn't want to. So don't rush him to the crib as soon as he knocks off six ounces of milk. All you'll get are screams. It's not sleep he's after, it's you. He wants to be stimulated; it's time to play and show off.

Unless you switch to his timetable, things are going to get stormy, especially during eating. This is when he'll really put on a show, such as swiping the spoon from you to feed himself. Actually he's practicing a new intellectual strategy called *prehension* which is the ability to coordinate the eyes and hands so that anything seen can be picked up. He may seem puffed up and a show-off as he boldly waves the spoon like a baton. But don't be a bully and wrench it from him. You might squash his feelings of competence, power, and control. These feelings are the core of his growing personality, which is marching side by side with his growing intellect.

Turning to the activities now, you will find some ideas to make playing with your baby more fun and more worthwhile.

13. LIP-LICKING

After packing away a gigantic lunch, there lay Erik with a tummy so round that it ballooned out of his little T-shirt. Yet his lip-licking suggested that he was still hungry. But when I brought additional food, he refused it. What more did he want? As lip-licking continued, I grew impatient and confused when the baby snubbed all offers of food.

Meal times could easily become one of your most trying situations, if you didn't realize that this form of lip-licking stems not from hunger, but from a new intellectual accomplishment: control over his reflexes.

Earlier, when touched or stimulated, the lips would automatically start sucking. But now the baby's mind is so powerful that such a reflex can be regulated. Along with this new power comes self-pride as your baby shares his new achievement with you.

Thus, lip-licking seems like an invitation. The baby seems to want to share with you and engage you.

Accept his invitation; try playing with him.

Touch his lips with your finger. At first, does he suck it? Then does his tongue begin licking? If you keep tapping his lips, does he lick more? What happens when you stop playing? Does his licking change in any way to attract your attention?

Keep in mind that the purpose of this play is to see if your baby's mind can control the sucking reflex. The sooner your baby gains control over such reflexes, the easier it will be for him to find out about himself. During Stage 3, in Activity 29, your baby will extend this control to the world around him.

DIARY

_____

_____

_____

_____

_____

GUIDE

See if the licking is any different when you touch your baby's lips with a toy. Does your finger or the toy induce more licking? Which arouses him more?

14. DROOLING

"What a slob!" I can still remember thinking this after having changed Christopher for what seemed to be the zillionth time. And then, like clockwork, he would come right back drooling and slobbering all over his newly changed top. Rather than just blotting dry his little shirt, I would again go through the whole changing routine. Clearly, I knew very little about child care and even less about child development and the significance of drooling.

Far from being a slob or even from being antagonistic, Christopher was demonstrating, through drooling, a simple understanding of such concepts as time, water density, space, viscosity, and distance. Although earlier, he had drooled all over himself, now he was gaining control—dangling the saliva like a fishing line, weighing each moment, calculating the tension, and just before it was out of control, snapping the saliva safely up into his mouth. Obviously a baby doesn't understand about space, time, tension, and the like as we do. Still, the drooling lays the primitive framework upon which these concepts will be built during adulthood.

If you are neat as a pin and expect your baby to be so too, try to back off a bit. Drooling, like other seemingly messy behaviors, contains many of the elements necessary for optimal intellectual growth. Let your baby explore; let him be a baby.

Sometimes a baby drools more with certain liquids than with others. Give your baby some sugar water. Is there any drooling? Does he blow bubbles? This is a more complex form of saliva play. Try milk or a little juice. What happens with cold and with warm water? The milk and juice are nutritional. Do they cause more drooling than the non-nutritional waters?

The drooling shows that your baby has developed enough control to attempt precise experiments. With this precise control, he's learning how to manipulate variables such as suspending the saliva for a certain length of time or for different time intervals. Activity 31 will require a more advanced form of this manipulation.

DIARY

GUIDE

Unlike lip-licking, drooling seems to be a private form of play for the baby's own amusement. Does he abandon the drooling and appear startled if you poke at him? Does your continued presence touch off his public form of play, lip-licking?

15. THUMB-SUCKING

"Babyish," grumbled one parent. "When do they stop it?" echoed another. These barbs were aimed at what may yet be the baby's most brazen display of control—thumb-sucking. For some adults, thumb-sucking is a deplorable habit, and the sooner it is broken, the better. Substitutes, such as pacifiers, are often employed to rescue the baby from thumb-sucking.

But watch what you are doing. Thumb-sucking is extremely important. It represents a new level of prehension as the baby can now start bringing things to her mouth. But just as significant, if not more critical, is that this act shows that, for the first time, your baby has complete control over something that can run contrary to your will. By sucking her thumb, the baby can challenge your authority, and a battle of wills may ensue.

Avoid the battle. Give in for your sake as well as the baby's. For her, thumb-sucking shows that the intellect is operating on a pretty advanced level. In contrast to the "Unwinding Stage", when the mind was limited to plodding along with only one idea at a time, now it can simultaneously coordinate many different ideas.

So don't get stuck on thumb-sucking. Use your time with the baby more constructively. Of course, if the thumb is raw, chewed, or mangled, take action. Otherwise, let it alone. If anything, you'll hamper her development of prehension—to say nothing of defeating your baby's self-confidence, which is so much a part of her development during "Self-discovery."

Let's take a look at how far thumb-sucking has progressed. During the last stage, when you held your baby out in front of you, her head began turning in the direction of her flapping hands, but that was the extent of her coordination.

Now hold your baby up in front of you, and see what happens. Do her hands calm down and approach her head? Is her head turned to one side, waiting for her hand? Does her hand make contact with her mouth? Does she force her thumb into her mouth? If so, this is a real sign of coordination and cognitive maturity.

Thumb-sucking is one of the early signs of eye–hand coordination. By following the above activity, this coordination will be strengthened and will soon lead to the development of *prehension*, that is, the ability to grab objects and bring them to the mouth or up to the eyes to be examined. Prehension will be fully developed at the end of "self-discovery."

DIARY

_____

_____

_____

_____

_____

_____

_____

GUIDE

For your baby's hand to move more efficiently, it must catch her eyes' attention; then the eye will guide the hand. Slip a bell or a little bracelet onto your baby's wrist. If this attracts her, her eyes will almost pop out of her head as they strain to guide her jerky and clumsy hand closer to her mouth.

16. A MOUTH FULL OF FINGERS

For weeks, it has been a steady uphill battle. Nevertheless, Erin is still hanging on, relentlessly struggling to inch her thumb closer to her mouth. Despite a few setbacks, each day sees more tension, discipline, and restraint poured into this effort. But just as it seems that the thumb is finally home free, Erin, either out of sheer joy or utter fatigue, momentarily lets down; and the thumb—like a balloon with air zipping out of it—fizzles, flops, and madly darts about until it lands way off target somewhere on her chin, nose, or cheek. She pauses, spits out the stray fingers that landed in her mouth, and then goes right back to work.

In the past, such a fiasco would have driven your baby to pull back her hand and start all over again. But now, in a flash of confidence, she stands her ground and builds on what she has already accomplished by carefully maneuvering her thumb off her cheek and into her mouth. Such efficient maneuvering, coupled with her new confidence and persistance, is just another example of how the mind and personality criss-cross to help your baby grow and develop.

As well as being a sign of a new intellectual coordination between the hand and mouth, thumb-sucking also serves your baby emotionally. When hungry, tired, cranky, or upset, she soothes and relaxes herself by plopping the old thumb in her mouth.

To determine how well developed her thumb sucking is, pull your baby's hand away from her mouth. Does she snap it right back? Or does she move her hand clumsily back to her mouth? Does she hold her head stationary, waiting for her hand? Or does she lean it anxiously towards her approaching thumb? Try this with her right and left hands. Is thumb-sucking equally developed in both?

When your baby can do these things, it will indicate that she has firmly developed hand–mouth coordination. If you try to help by placing your baby's thumb near her mouth, she'll interpret your assistance as interference. Don't do things for your baby that she can do on her own.

DIARY

_____

_____

_____

_____

_____

GUIDE

Sometimes a ribbon tied on your baby's wrist makes it easier for her to concentrate on bringing her hand to her mouth.

17. SMILES AND FROWNS

Let's face it. Although your baby is doing some fantastic things, nothing stacks up to the first time she turns, looks up, and smiles at you. It's heaven. We have had three kids, and the first smile never loses its magic. At first, you are almost in a spell, not knowing what to do; then your feelings take over, and you scoop up your baby to kiss, hug, and caress her as never before.

This is your payoff. After weeks of mixed feelings, doubts, and concerns, suddenly it has all been worth it. Your baby knows you and loves you. Often we are so struck by these smiles that a baby's other emotions go undetected. Yet these, too, are important to notice. A long empty gaze points to unsureness, while a chuckle and flapping arms indicate interest and motivation. If your baby is gripped by fear, drooping lips and a wrinkled brow map his face. And finally, indifference, tedium, or boredom is marked by a raised eyebrow, closed lips, and a passing glance.

In terms of cognitive development, smiling is yet another case of growing control and coordination, this time between the eyes and mouth. Now whatever is seen becomes translated into some emotional expression involving the mouth.

You can observe how much this coordination has progressed. Earlier, your baby smiled only if you used the following routine: moving around, talking or singing, and rocking your baby. Now try just one of these actions. Which causes the most smiling? Which the least? Are any of the actions ignored? Can just making eye contact with your baby cause a smile?

Remember, the intent of the routine is to discover just how many stimuli your baby needs before he'll smile. During Activity 43 more subtle signs of expressing feelings and awareness begin to develop.

DIARY

_____

_____

_____

_____

_____

_____

_____

GUIDE

Some babies may smile more for a toy than for people. Do certain shapes or colors, or the sounds of a favorite toy, produce smiles and laughter in your baby?

18. THE FORTUNETELLER

Any day now, as I did with Erin, you are going to glance over and catch your baby reading her palms. With the intensity and seriousness of a fortuneteller, there she'll be, poring over every detail and irregularity of her hand. Her concentration is so strong that her eyes seem locked to her hands. It is enough to make one believe that she can actually see the future within her hand. And in a way, she can. For the baby's future, as a learner, depends on coordinating the eyes and hands. The first step of this coordination is having eyes mature enough to focus on things, as is now the case.

Earlier, the eyes were flighty and danced around from one thing to the other. But now they can zoom ahead and lock into place. Although the eyes stay fixed to one place for long periods of time, nothing in the immediate environment escapes them; even slight movements on either side are instantly tracked, catalogued, and studied.

Not only does the range of your baby's vision increase but so does its sensitivity. Your baby can now begin to distinguish you from strangers, if not from other members of the family. This is especially true when she needs soothing; if someone other than you approaches, she'll cry even more.

What toys make your baby concentrate the most? A doll or a rattle? Shake the rattle. Does the sound plus the sight produce more concentration? Swing the doll and rattle. Now what's her reaction?

This is the type of mental coordination that distinguishes "Self-Discovery" from the "Unwinding Stage". The baby is trying to coordinate her eyes and hands, and her eyes and her ears. In so doing, she is beginning to discover more and more things about herself.

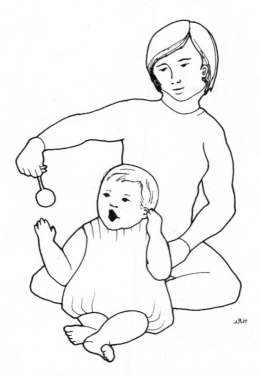

All this attention to hands will pay off. Soon, in Stage 3, you'll see how discriminating your baby's hands have become—as is shown by Activity 32.

DIARY

_____

_____

_____

_____

_____

_____

GUIDE

Some babies will not focus on a toy when a parent is in the same field of vision—they prefer to look at you. While out of sight, dangle the toy over your baby's head. Now is there a different reaction?

19. THE MONSTER

I had just stepped out of the shower with a big towel wrapped in turban fashion around my head when Erik looked up, startled, and screamed. As I raced to him, the turban unraveled; and before it slipped to the floor his crying ceased, only to be replaced by a puzzled look on his face. In no time, his face melted into a smile. As far as he was concerned, I had just turned from a monster into his Daddy.

Like most babies during this stage, Erik was terrified by viewing something incongruous. The turban somewhat changed my appearance —as might a wig, sun glasses, a shower cap, or my face lathered with shaving cream. To Erik, such moderate alterations would change my looks. But I was not totally changed: Simultaneously, I was both Daddy and not Daddy. Unable to handle this incongruity, the baby breaks down emotionally and cries.

Intellectually, this inability to handle incongruous situations points out how rigid your baby's thinking really is: Ideas and concepts once formed can't be changed. For example, his idea of daddy contains many parts, and if there is a change in one, such as a turban for hair, he can't incorporate this change.

Along with incongruities, the baby in this stage finds it hard to incorporate novelty into his thinking.

Take an aluminum pie plate or the lid from a big pot and hold it at arm's length from your baby. Does he stare at it? If so, this indicates an element of curiosity. Is there any sucking or swallowing? This would signal that your baby has gone beyond curiosity and is now interested in the object. Move the plate halfway to your baby. Does he back off? Now he may be getting leery; his mind can't cope with this new object.

What you're observing during this play is how your baby reacts to new ideas. It won't be until Stage 3 that he begins to adapt to different objects, as is illustrated in Activity 33.

DIARY

_____

_____

_____

_____

_____

_____

_____

_____

GUIDE

While this novel object is halfway from him, your baby can take time mulling over this new thing and trying to see where it fits in his mind. However, if it's moved too close, it's on top of him before he's made up his mind; and this might provoke several reactions, such as grimacing, thrashing wildly, or simply turning away indifferently. How did your baby respond?

20. THE CRYING GAME

If you get caught in the crying game, it can be murder on your nerves. Christopher lured us into it early. It started outside his room as we anxiously waited and listened to a squall of crying that drifted into a silent calm only to start up again abruptly. It was touch and go on our part, not knowing whether to go in or stay out, wondering if he really needed us or whether he was just on the verge of falling asleep.

What Christopher was up to was learning to coordinate his crying or early vocalizations with hearing. Later, such a coordination will enable your child to engage in dialogues in which he listens to someone and then responds. However, now he's merely beginning to understand that the sounds being heard are his own. So your baby takes great delight in listening to his crying and then turning it off, causing silence. Even if the yelling and crying are based on real pain, often the baby will override such discomfort in order to practice this new coordination. That is why it is always best to check your baby rather than trying to play a game or to outguess him.

Parents are not totally innocent. We also play games with our babies like the "Hey look" one, which uses a combination of sights and sounds to distract a cranky, whining, or stubborn baby. This distraction is possible only because of a newly developed coordination between your baby's hearing and vision. Now he will turn and look at what he hears.

Shake a bell to your baby's side. Does he turn and look? Make a noise behind him. What happens? Does he merely glance over his shoulder? Or does your baby twist his whole body around in order to make a thorough search for the sound? The more he moves his body, the more advanced his coordination is.

This activity shows how your baby will respond with both his eyes and ears to the slightest sound. The ability to coordinate two functions, such as vision and hearing, is the hallmark of this stage.

DIARY

_____

_____

_____

_____

_____

_____

GUIDE

Some babies will not look for the sound unless they first see the bell. So show your baby the bell before you bring it to his side or behind him to shake it. Does such a procedure help your baby search for the sound?

21. CHOO-CHOOS AND BOW-WOWS

Erin was our third baby to come along, making this the third consecutive year I was saddled with reading about "Choo-choos" and "Bow-wows." Believe me, it was wearing thin. Knowing language would not surface for quite a few months, I could not see the point to this reading. Then one afternoon we heard a puppy yelping, and a quizzical look gripped Erin's face—a look that immediately vanished as soon as I said, "Bow-wow." Evidently, she knew what I was saying. Erin was able to associate the familiar symbol for dog, "Bow-wow," with the unfamiliar yelping sound.

Intellectually, she is now able to classify sounds and words into such categories as familiar, unfamiliar, interesting, and strange. One familiar sound she can respond to is her name. It is not only sounds and names, but also tones and qualities, that your baby can recognize. So watch your intonations, for even at this early age, your baby can discern the subtle feelings and emotional changes connoted by speech.

At this time, babies are especially alert to strange sounds. Make a strange noise by dropping a shoe on the floor. What is her reaction? A blank stare or trance? If something familiar like your voice breaks into her trance, is she relieved? Then does she smile? Your baby connects certain feelings with certain voices. Whose voices generally make her smile, laugh, or giggle? How does she respond to the different voices of family members? If a radio is turned on, what is your baby's reaction?

When your baby responds differently to different sounds, it's an example of her ability to classify. Although she can only classify sounds now, later, in the following stage, your baby will be able to produce intelligible syllables. See Activity 47.

DIARY

_____

_____

_____

_____

_____

_____

_____

_____

_____

GUIDE

Being interested and curious about new sounds is the next step in your baby's development. Take her favorite old toy and make noises with it by rubbing, banging, or shaking it. Do the same with a new toy and note her reaction.

22. A CHIP OFF THE OLD BLOCK

Have you ever heard exchanges like these between in-laws? "Erin's smile definitely comes from our side"; "When cross, Erik looks just like Steve"; "He's a chip off the old block." Such comments are routinely dismissed by parents as being prompted merely by family loyalties. Don't be so quick to dismiss such remarks; they may contain some real insights. For at this time, babies are mostly imitating only their parents; hence the family resemblance.

Earlier, through contagion and mutual imitation, your baby would imitate virtually anyone. But now, he's selective. If surrounded by a bunch of people making various noises, a baby will select out his parents' voices to imitate, and on other occasions he will imitate their smiles, grimaces, frowns, and so on.

The fact that parents are preferred as models to imitate reflects two developments: first, a strong emotional attachment to you; and second, a growing mental capacity to separate out, from all other actions, your behavior—which is then copied exactly. This is called *accommodation;* it is an intellectual ability that helps the mind adapt and conform to the outside world.

To observe the workings of accommodation, nod your head up and down. Does your baby immediately start nodding? Or does he wait until you stop? The latter shows accommodation: your baby is deliberately studying your moves. In fact, as you are nodding, notice whether your baby's head is shaking slightly. If it is, this means that he is practicing in order to achieve a perfect imitation of your action.

Next, wag your head back and forth. Does your baby copy your wagging immediately? Or does he wait? Can you catch him practicing at all?

Your baby can only make gross imitations using his head now. Eventually, as shown in Activity 46, your baby will be able to perform imitations involving other parts of his body.

DIARY

_____

_____

_____

_____

_____

GUIDE

If your baby can easily accommodate to head imitations, see if he can do the same for your voice. Start singing up the scale. Does he raise his voice with each successive sound you utter?

23. THE FACE JOB

What's coming next can conservatively be called fantastic, if not stupendous. How else could eye–hand coordination, or prehension, be rated? Soon your baby will be able to grab whatever is in reach and bring it not just to his mouth, but to his eyes. As never before, your baby will learn, as you do, by visual examination rather than by sucking. The corner has been turned. Your baby is on his way to learning through manipulation and experimentation—the forerunners of adult logical thinking.

Like most grand accomplishments, prehension starts out quite simply—as a grasping reflex—during "Unwinding". At that time, a touch on Christopher's palm was needed to trigger any grasping or holding; otherwise his hands were limp, having no activity of their own. Without self-activity, the baby's hands lay dormant and unnoticed by him. It's only now that the baby notices his hands. This marks the first step in the development of prehension.

Later we will examine other steps: the "Poke in the Eye," which is a basic sign of simple eye–hand coordination; the "Human Vacuum Cleaner," in which your baby blindly jams everything into his mouth, illustrating hand–mouth coordination; and the "Spoon Feud," which shows how vision is becoming the controlling force in prehension.

Before getting too far ahead, let's return to that first step: the hands becoming more active and more noticed. What the hands initially grasp, or at least what's most conspicuous, are the different parts of the face. How common it is to see Christopher pulling his lips, chin, and ear, or scratching his head and nose.

Here's a good example of your baby discovering things about himself through manual exploration. Some parents get alarmed, fearing that the baby's face may be marred or seriously scratched. Obviously, caution should be exercised. You may want to show your baby his reflection in a mirror in order to help him discover himself. But don't rely solely on the mirror. The baby basically learns about himself through exploring with his hands. Consider what is going on: The hands, which during "Unwinding" could never act by themselves, are now on their own, racing around the face, smoothing every bump, dimple, and crease, ready to plug any opening—be it the nostril, mouth, or ear.

Earlier, when still awkward and slow, your baby's hand could be activated only if his palm were bluntly stimulated or touched. Now, just brushing his fingers is enough to start his hands churning and grabbing.

Try brushing his fingers with a napkin. Does he grab it? Do all his fingers have to be stimulated? Next, try a rattle. Do you observe the same responses? Does he grab the toy and hold it just momentarily or does he hold it for an entire minute or more? What kinds of objects does he hold for the longest time?

If your baby's hands react to the slightest touch, this demonstrates that prehension is ready to develop. This increased sensitivity to touch, is a clear-cut example that your baby is acquiring more control over himself. As your baby gains more control over his entire body, he will be able to unleash all kinds of power in order to cause things to happen. Activity 38 shows how your baby tries to use pure force and energy in order to bring about changes.

DIARY

_____

_____

_____

_____

_____

GUIDE

Try toys of different shapes and textures to see if some are easier for him to hold and grasp than others. Hand him a washcloth, a block, a straw, and so on. Which one does he handle most easily?

24. A POKE IN THE EYE

If you missed your baby's nose-scratching and ear-pulling, then it's a sure bet that you'll miss the next sign of his developing prehension, rubbing his eyes. No doubt such rubbing indicates fatigue when accompanied by stretching and yawning. However, in the absence of these two actions, it signals simple eye–hand coordination. Earlier, the eyes and hands were uncoordinated, often resulting in the baby's poking herself in the eye. But now she blinks and shuts her eye just before it is poked—a sure sign of a budding relationship between her eyes and hands.

Increasingly, the eyes grow more attached to the hands, following them everywhere. The baby is entranced by their actions—by their rubbing, clasping, and squeezing one another. Equally fascinating to

her is thumb-sucking, a hand–mouth coordination upon which the ultimate coordination of the eyes and hand is built. Although the thumb can be sucked, toys cannot. Despite this, she's captivated by toys as her hands manipulate them and move them around. In fact, the more she watches these various hand movements, the faster prehension develops.

To help make your baby's hands more attractive, try the following: Cover her hands with a napkin. Will your baby look for them? Dangle your hand in front of her eyes. Does this prompt a search for her own hand? Does she grab your hand, as if mistaking it for her own hand? Make your baby a little bracelet with strands of various colored yarn. Is she more attracted to her hands now?

The aim of this activity is to give your baby practice at eye–hand coordination. She's now beginning to anticipate the movement of her hands. As will be shown in Activity 44, this ability to anticipate becomes refined later.

DIARY

_____

_____

_____

_____

_____

_____

_____

_____

GUIDE

Prehension has one drawback at this time. Your baby can grab only those toys that are in the same line of vision as her hands. Start shaking a rattle in front of your baby and gradually move it towards her hand. How close to her hand must the rattle approach before she grabs it? Does she grab the rattle at a point further and further from her hand each time you try this guide?

25. THE VACUUM CLEANER

Sucking pins, chewing up buttons, slurping ointment, and swallowing body waste.

This is not a garbage disposal; but it might be your baby, who's become a menace—a human vacuum cleaner, capable of sucking anything that's grabbed. Once, only the thumb could be sucked. Now that hand–mouth coordination is possible, anything your baby grasps is brought to his mouth and sucked on.

Since so many inedible objects, such as pins, buttons, and the like, abound in the baby's little world, parents are pressed into censoring his play things, often to the extreme of taking all toys from him. Yet some toys must remain, because his hands and mouth need objects to practice with, for this coordination is still shaky and rough.

To gauge how refined the coordination is, try the following. Rub the side of his hand lightly with a toy. How does he pick it up? By firmly holding the toy in his palm? Or loosely, with only his finger tips? The second method shows that he needs more practice. When he holds the rattle loosely, it's not balanced well and usually tips out of his hand. If he holds the toy, does he carry it to his mouth in one smooth motion? Or is it jerky? Supply your baby with big toys, such as blocks, for big toys require a firm grip and, unlike small buttons, they can't be swallowed.

Earlier, your baby could only suck his thumb, but now he's learning to bring other objects to his mouth. It takes time to develop this form of hand–mouth coordination; but once he has it, your baby uses it to show off. He'll suck anything. So watch what you leave around. In fact, it may be wise to keep some parts of the house off limits for the baby at this stage.

DIARY

_____

_____

_____

_____

_____

GUIDE

If you don't rub his hand, can he still grab the toy? It seems, at this point, that a toy must be touched, not just seen, in order for the baby to pick it up.

26. THE SPOON FEUD

"Open your mouth!" "What's wrong?" "Aren't you hungry?" "Give me the spoon!" "Where are your manners?" Such were the demands we were leveling at Erik as feeding suddenly turned into a feud.

At the center of this madness is the spoon: You want it in her mouth, and she wants it outside to stare at. This passion for looking and staring is so powerful that it takes preference over everything else. So to get the spoon where it can be best seen, your baby resorts to any means: clamping shut the mouth to bar entrance, chomping down and capturing the spoon if it does gain access, or simply yanking the spoon from the mouth.

None of this is done to annoy you, but to examine and study the spoon visually. To make things easier, give the baby a spoon of her own to examine. This will be helpful for her learning. Her interest, at this point in development, has shifted from the mouth to the eyes. She no longer sucks things but rather she carefully inspects, reads, and scans them much in the same manner as adults do when attempting to understand or analyze a problem. In a sense, your baby has adopted your learning style. She seems more reflective than reflexive, or more prone to analyze things carefully than to jam them impulsively in her mouth.

Although we have dwelt on the spoon, in no way have we singled it out. Anything approaching the face is dealt with in the same manner: It is studied rather than sucked.

Hold a doll in front of your baby. Does she stare at it? Does she make any attempt to grab the toy? If her attempts are awkward, then brush the doll across her hands. Now does she look attentively at the toy and at her hand? Do you get the impression that she's trying to coach her hand closer to the doll? In all likelihood she won't grab the toy; you will have to hand it to her. When you hand her the doll, does she suck it or study it? Does she suck it momentarily and then withdraw it to be scanned and inspected?

The point of this activity is to observe whether the baby resorts to her old behavior of merely sucking objects or whether she now brings them close to her eyes to be studied. In Activity 41, she'll start using spoons and other instruments in order to learn about cause and effect.

DIARY

_____

_____

_____

_____

_____

GUIDE

There's still a big snag in this new development. Although the eyes are ready for it, the hands are unprepared. If anything, the hands appear caught between the old and new style. As a result, toys are not brought to the eyes but are held down near the mouth. Although not sucked, they are still obscured from complete visual examination.

To help your baby maintain visual contact, hand her a toy and then push her arm up to eye level. Can she keep it at this level? Or does she drop it to the mouth?

27. ALL EYES

Although your baby has been making steady progress in developing prehension, something has been left out. Your baby can only pick up those things he can touch. If he sees an object he can't pick it up unless his hand is also in his line of vision. Your baby does not coordinate his eyes and hand; rather, like a person groping and stumbling in the dark, he occasionally bumps into things, and then he picks them up. Aside from these accidents, your baby has been totally dependent on you for his supply of toys and other objects.

Now his eyes are starting to take charge as they alternately look between the hand and toy. With each glance, his hand drags a little closer to the toy. Finally, when both the hand and the toy are in the same line of vision, your baby can grab the toy.

Although clumsy and shaky, these actions stand as a landmark in your baby's development, for at no other time have his eyes guided his hands. Now, on his own, he can gather in toys and other objects; and when he plays with these, his actions lead to intellectual growth. Prior to this, you were the chief supplier of such toys. Now, in this area at least, he has independence, independence that brings him feelings of confidence, pride, and productivity.

Observe this process unfold by shaking a rattle as you place it just within your baby's reach. Does he start glancing? Look at his head. Is it straining and nodding? Does it appear that he's pulling his hand with his eyes? Does he glare at his hands too long, thus forgetting, and losing sight of, the toy? To re-establish his glancing, brush the toy across his hand. Now does he start moving his hand? Does he bring the toy to his mouth or to his eyes once he's grabbed it?

By playing with your baby in this manner, you're trying to observe if he has to see the object and his hand together before he can pick up the object. Your baby is learning how to make contact with an object. Activity 39 is a good example of how much progress will eventually be made in this area.

DIARY

_____

_____

_____

_____

_____

_____

_____

GUIDE

The next development in prehension comes when your baby can glare at his hands without forgetting the toy. This shows that your baby can retain some image of the object while concentrating solely on his hands. Vary the distance between the toy and his hand. As the toy gets closer to his hand, does he tend to glare more at his hand or at the toy? Or does he continue to glance equally at both?

28. WHAT PEOPLE THINK

When people think of a baby beginning to learn, they think of her starting to use language. When people think of her growing independent, they think of the baby walking and getting around on her own. And when they think of a baby effortlessly picking up a toy, they think little of it. Yet this act of prehension, as discussed earlier, opens your baby to independence as well as to advanced levels of learning.

Whereas in the past prehension was strained and rough, now it is accomplished with ease. No longer do the hands have to be coached and directed by the eyes. Your baby is finally free from such awkwardness, the last obstacle to complete eye–hand coordination. From here on, anything that she sees can be brought up to her eyes for examination and study. Also, objects need not be in the same line of vision as the hand for this coordination to work. Now, merely upon seeing a toy, she forms an idea that instantly presses her hands into action.

Coordinating her actions is only one part of this present development. Your baby can also mesh two ideas together at the same time. For example, your baby can seem to be totally absorbed with a toy when, slyly, she begins searching for another object that's suddenly crossed her mind. Or she'll be extremely diplomatic with you, playing and laughing, while in the back of her mind she's considering what she'll do when you leave. As with her eyes and hands, she can also simultaneously coordinate two ideas or divide her attention between two things.

To determine how well prehension is operating, distract your baby momentarily while slipping a toy into her hand. Does she stare at the toy? Or does she nonchalantly carry it up to her eyes? Distract her again, but this time shake a rattle. Does she look up from her distraction? Or does she merely send out her hands, searching for the rattle? If the latter happens, it is a sign that her attention and thinking are divided between the distraction and the rattle.

Now your baby has completed eye–hand coordination. She no longer has to see an object in order to pick it up. She thinks her hands can solve any problem. This power goes to her head, as you will see in Activity 30.

DIARY

_____

_____

_____

_____

_____

_____

_____

_____

GUIDE

One limit of prehension is that it can't deal with objects at a distance. Try holding a toy out of your baby's reach. Without realizing the distance, she will still try to snatch it effortlessly. Failing, she becomes anxious and starts thumb-sucking or smacking her lips. Distance or far space is a concept that will continue to trouble her over the next few months.

But, on the bright side, prehension has been fully mastered. As a result, your baby is more self-reliant, independent, and better able to analyze her world. These are characteristics which ready her for the next stage of infant development, "Finding His Surroundings."

FINDING HIS SURROUNDINGS

Four to Ten Months

Hold on to your sanity and grab your sense of humor, for a real test is descending upon you. Remember that calm, quiet, little baby who bubbled with coos and smiles? Well, in her place, during the next few months, is going to appear a self-centered, cocky, know-it-all.

Don't get me wrong; she isn't malicious. If anything, she's funny. It's simply the manner of most babies during this stage to feel that they are in complete control of everything. However, this power is illusion, since most of her actions are plagued by magical thinking, or the perception that things can be made to happen by merely waving one's arms. That's why it takes time for her even to learn how to play with something as easy as a rattle. The fact is that she has less control now than she did during "Self-Discovery."

"Self-Discovery" brought prehension and the conviction that the hands were the supreme power that governed all learning. So for the time being, at least, the possibility that anything else like the arms, head, torso, or legs might also have similar power remained only an idle fancy in the baby's mind. Such fancies were never treated seriously during "Self-Discovery", for the baby was content merely to master near space, that is, anything within hands' reach. Soon this contentment faded as the baby sought to explore and control those things beyond reach in far space. The urge to explore led to this new stage of "finding her surroundings."

Having the inclination to explore was fine, but what could really be accomplished without first developing some new abilities? Sure, the eight month old baby could stand and reach things, creep and crawl to distant objects. Still, anything too high or anything in far space remained beyond control. That is, it did until the day your baby, while frantically trying to reach the crib's mobile by flagging his arms and stretching his legs, accidently struck the head board, sending shock waves up to the mobile. What followed stunned him. There was the mobile, fluttering and swaying without having been touched. Then he hit upon the idea that far space could be controlled, explored, and manipulated merely by strenuous waving, kicking, and bouncing. Here lies the root of the *magical thinking* that is to rule your baby's actions for the next several months.

What was an idle consideration a few weeks ago suddenly sweeps your baby into ways of thinking and feeling. Fantasies about the power lurking in his arms, legs, and torso had actually come true. If anything, these wild magical gyrations seem to surpass even his wildest dreams. As such, it's easy to see how all this could go to his head, leading your baby to perceive himself as absolutely powerful and authoritative to the extent that he begins to defy you in many ways. He shakes his head "No-No" on seeing the bottle since now, because he is teething, he prefers solids; he pushes himself from you because he can sit alone; he protests if a toy is removed; and he refuses to surrender a blanket or pillow that may need washing. Realizing that the baby is not mean or fresh but rather that he is acting out of an intellectual pride should temper your reactions to his challenges.

Since he has fallen into magical thinking by chance, it seems fitting that your baby's first step out of such thinking should also be an accident. This first step probably occurred during one of your baby's wild flings in which a stick she was brandishing unintentionally knocked down a toy from a high shelf. This act of hitting and making contact with a distant object must have been continually repeated until the baby saw a connection between contact and causality. Other experiences, such as pulling toys on a string or hitting objects with a spoon, must have forced your baby to admit how much more efficient these instruments were for dealing with her surroundings than were her frantic kicking and bouncing. With this admission, the next step follows naturally—that is the recognition of just how efficient and helpful people can be to her.

This marks a turnabout. Now your baby begins to cut away her cocky self-centeredness and grow more social. This attitude shows up in her language imitation, but more especially in her play, as she revels with you in such games as "Sooooo Big," "Pop Goes the Weasel," and "Peek-A-Boo."

In summary, this new stage opens your baby to a far off world that was once closed to her. This journey from near space to far space hinges on a number of developments. Physically, your baby has to be able to crawl, creep, and stand. Intellectually, she has to reason on a more logical and less magical plane. And finally, her personality has to change from a self-centered, cocky, outlook to one that is sensitive as well as socially attuned to people. As these developments gradually come about over the next six months your baby will be better able to understand the world around her.

29. THE RATTLE

If there is one toy that is synonymous with infancy, it's the rattle. It took Christopher months before he learned how to play with this toy properly. Sure, your baby can shake the rattle; but he has no idea that he is causing the noise. In fact, as it rattles, he looks amazed—if not bewildered. If by chance you happen by, he nods and smiles, as if thanking you for the noise.

Up to this point your baby's major concern is still himself, not the toys in his surroundings. It never crossed Christopher's mind that such toys could be made to rattle, jingle, or squeak. Farthest from his thinking was the idea that he had control over the sounds he heard. Toys were considered simply as objects to be either looked at, held, or sucked.

This egocentric or self-centered view changes over the next few months as your baby moves out and tinkers with the world around him. The shift from himself to the outside world is the main push of this third stage.

See if your baby is making any progress in this shift. Give him a rattle. Does he shake it? What's his reaction? Does he look at you? Perhaps he just scans his surroundings. Does he ever examine the rattle?

The point of this activity is to see if your baby realizes that his hands are causing the toy to rattle. Your baby is truly naive at this stage of development. He's just starting to grasp the idea that he can affect things around him.

DIARY

GUIDE

Often the rattling is so startling that your baby lets go of the toy and ends up shaking an empty hand. To help him make the connection between shaking a toy and producing a noise, slip a bracelet made out of yarn, with a little bell attached to it, onto his wrist. The bracelet can't be dropped; and the bell should be enough of an attention-grabber that he'll spend a lot of time studying the bracelet and his wrist.

30. THE BATH

Gather some big towels, put on a raincoat, and clear the area. You are not preparing for a mighty storm, you are merely preparing to bathe your baby. If yours is anything like Erik, who furiously beat, pounded, and splashed his bath water into a tidal wave, then the reason for this elaborate preparation is obvious.

What's not as obvious is the reason why all this frantic pounding happens in the first place. Could it be that your baby simply loves the water? Well, that's all right for an adult answer. But from the baby's point of view, all this wild arm-flailing and bouncing around is the key to causality. The more commotion he causes, the more happens. Just with a few zealous shakes and bounces in his crib, he can cause you to come running or make toys spill out onto the floor—to say nothing of the earthquake-like tremors he can set rumbling through his crib.

Such wild carryings-on are not intended to be harmful. Yet a curtain carelessly draped over the headboard of a crib or a hastily fastened mobile could shake loose and possibly fall on your baby, smothering or hurting him. So be cautious: Be aware that potentially dangerous things such as ointments, oils, and diaper pins must be completely removed from the immediate area, for even if such objects are just placed out of your baby's reach, his wild gyrations could easily move them within his reach.

If your baby were concerned only with causing things to vibrate or fall, then his view of causality would be appropriate. However, the thrust of this current stage is to understand and analyze all the little working parts of the environment, such as rattles, blankets, sheets, and dolls. So what is required is that these explosive movements be channeled and toned down. In this way your baby will have the opportunity to calmly and patiently examine the special qualities of every object encountered.

One way to tone down these movements is to focus your baby's attention only on the exact behaviors that cause certain actions. You can do this with a rattle by wrapping a large wad of tape around its handle. When the handle is heavy, your baby is bound to take notice of his one hand holding the rattle and eventually realize that it alone is causing the shaking. He'll realize that neither his other hand nor his bouncing torso and kicking legs have anything to do with the shaking movement.

After a few shakes does your baby stop and study this taped-up rattle? Does he shake it any differently? Does his empty hand stop shaking? Does he bounce less?

As your baby plays, you're trying to determine if he sees the relationship between the toy rattling and the specific movement of his hand. Your baby will continue to make definite progress in concentrating on his hands as they explore different objects. Activity 51 will soon point out the progress your baby is making in this area.

DIARY

_____

_____

_____

_____

_____

GUIDE

Because your baby often shakes with all his might, the heavy rattle could go unnoticed. If so, then muffle the rattle by taping up its bulb. The change in noise, along with the heavy handle, should draw your baby's attention to the toy and to his hand.

31. PUNCHING, JABBING, AND SLAPPING

A wild slap with a quick jab, followed by a flurry of punches, sounds like a boxing match; but in this case, it's a commentary on Erin's new development. Along with shaking as a means for causing different effects upon toys, she is also learning punches, jabs, and slaps.

Although unleashed with force and determination, these new behaviors in no way mirror feelings of aggression or meanness. They simply show how intellectually determined your baby is becoming. For example, if there's a toy dangling within reach, she can shake it to experiment with sounds; slap it to examine its arc; or punch it to study its strength and resilience.

Punching can be started by challenging your baby with a toy. Hold a rattle on a string above her. Lower the toy and then quickly reel it in. As it slips through her hand, she will tap or slap it with her fingers—two behaviors pretty close to punching and jabbing.

How many challenges does it take for punching or jabbing to result? Dangle the rattle over her. Does she grab, shake, or punch it? While it is dangling, bounce the toy off her knuckles or finger tips. Now what happens? Does her body shake and twist while she's punching?

What you're trying to do is to get the baby to expand her actions. During Activity 65, you can observe how easily she expands her actions and varies them with different toys.

DIARY

_____

_____

_____

_____

_____

_____

GUIDE

If your baby doesn't slap, jab, or punch the rattle, swing it toward her hands like a tease. This may cause her to strike out at the toy.

32. THE PICKPOCKET

We first noticed this behavior in Erin. If, while in the crib, she accidentally kicked the rattle, her fingers would race speedily along the blanket, dodging everything else, until they reached the toy.

Like a pickpocket, your baby is gradually developing a deft touch. In the past, her hands were blunt and clumsy, lacking any real power to discriminate. If she heard a rattle, your baby would merely shake the first thing touched, whether a doll or blanket, mistaking these for the rattle. She couldn't connect her touch to what she was hearing.

Now, if this same sound rings out, she'll make an exhaustive search and won't settle for anything but the rattle. Often when this reasonable approach fails, your baby drops back to the more primitive large hand-waves and body-bounces and kicks. Although they don't yield the rattle, such waves and bounces usually draw you onto the scene. Confused as to your baby's specific wants, your temper begins to rise and rise as she soundly rejects each toy you offer. Before things get too out of hand, pick up your baby and walk around. This should distract, if not soothe, both of you.

Observe your baby's new touch in action. While distracting your baby, ring a bell and then put it down in a pool of other objects—all within arms' reach. Does she waste time fingering the other objects? When she grasps the bell, what is her reaction? One of surprise? Does she stop waving her empty hand? Does she shake the bell in a smooth and even manner? Does she blink before she shakes the bell? If so, this is a sign of anticipation. As with adults, anticipation comes only when a baby is in full control of a situation and knows what to expect next.

The purpose of this activity is to see how well your baby discriminates by touch. Progress in this discrimination will really be seen in Activity 64.

DIARY

_____

_____

_____

_____

_____

_____

GUIDE

If it is plain that your baby has no trouble discriminating the bell from a doll, blanket, or block, then try something a little harder. This time, while distracting your baby, shake a rattle. Then immediately stick it in a pile of other toys that all feel like the rattle's handle: a crayon, a toothbrush, and a clothespin. Does she still discriminate easily?

33. DUMPING CEREAL IN THE HAIR

At birth, Christopher was about as fat as a guitar string, but he made up for it with a head of hair that looked like a fifteen pound bale of barbed wire. It was always a conversation piece for us, but Christopher had hardly noticed it until lately. Now our baby's favorite pastime was running his fingers through this tangle of fibers. However, this soon lost its kick, so Christopher resorted to dumping bowls of cereal into his hair and then weaving and burrowing his fingers through this congealing mess.

It took two more babies before we realized that Christopher was not punishing us, rejecting his cereal, or defoliating his scalp. He was simply practicing a new skill known as *accommodation*. With this skill a baby learns to fit his behaviors to different objects. Having mastered the intricate channels of his bushy hair, Christopher sought a new challenge: Could his fingers accommodate to the sticky paste-like mixture of hair and cereal?

This isn't an alibi or an attempt to give lofty explanations for the bothersome things a baby does. Just look at your baby's play. Before, toys were either knocked silly or clutched as if they were frozen to his hand. Now there seems to be a middle of the road approach. He plays with toys at a slower pace. Although conservative, this pace allows your baby to find the right way to handle his toys.

Place a ball in your open palm, and extend it to the baby. Does he push the ball off your palm? If so, was it a clumsy act, or was it a hard blow? Put the ball back in your palm. Does he knock it off once more? Does he alternate between slapping it away and nudging it? Or does he take the middle road and gingerly pick up the ball?

Here your baby is trying to adapt his actions so that they fit the toy. Often these attempts at adaptation are overridden by his self-centeredness, the general personality trait of this stage.

DIARY

_____

_____

_____

_____

_____

GUIDE

Since a ball rolls easily, substitute a block. Such a toy is not as sensitive to touch as a ball, so it better resists your baby's clumsy or miscalculated gestures.

34. CRINKLES

Parents often wonder what kinds of toys to buy for babies. For now, forget the toys. Just give your baby the tissue paper they come wrapped in. She'll crinkle, squeeze, crush, and rip the paper with more delight and fascination than if you had given her a toy.

At this point, your baby is developing small or fine motor behaviors, such as crinkling, which differs from the bigger gross actions found in shaking, pushing, and slapping.

With such nimbleness, many things are possible, such as picking up crumbs and other debris. Therefore this is not the time to become lax about cleaning up tobacco strands, cigarette butts, paint flakes, pins, needles, and the like, because now your baby can easily pick up these things and plop them in her mouth.

However, there are advantages to these fine motor acts. They do reflect a precise and calculating mind capable of studying and examining every little detail of the immediate environment.

Contrast the windmill arm motions of punching and slapping with the measured movement of these fine motor acts. The hands and fingers have become more than just blind forces; now, they seem to bend or accommodate in order to fit the object. The baby realizes that only the slightest pressure or twist is enough to cause a certain reaction in the object. For example she no longer pounds her rubber duck to make it squeak; she understands that the toy need only be squeezed.

Hand your baby a piece of cellophane paper. Does she study it? Does she seem serious? Does she immediately crush the paper? Or does she gradually crinkle it? Does she open and close it like an accordion? In how many different ways does she handle the paper? Can she unravel it?

The cellophane is a good prop because it provides feedback. It allows the baby to analyze each of her manipulations carefully. If she learns something new during her actions, the baby can now pinpoint when and where this new learning occurred. In Activity 53 you'll be able to observe your baby using feedback to correct her actions.

DIARY

_____

_____

_____

_____

_____

GUIDE

To see if these fine motor acts are really developed, weave some yarn in between your baby's fingers. Can she easily untangle this mess?

35. COCKSURE

Without doubt, your baby has been covering a lot of ground lately, such as creeping and crawling, to say nothing of recent mental developments. New horizons have been opening for her. And if you are not impressed, she certainly is—to the extent of being cocksure. Your baby feels she's at the peak of her development and there's nothing futher to learn. Now she thinks there's only one way to act: to follow her proven and successful ways of the past. In a sense there's nothing new under the sun. That goes for anything, especially new toys, which are treated just like old ones.

Get something new, something your baby has had little exposure to, such as a big envelope. Demonstrate a new behavior by opening and closing the envelope before handing it to your baby. Does she try these new behaviors herself? Or does she treat the envelope in the old fashion, by crinkling and squeezing it? Perhaps she just stares at it?

At this point, new things are not exciting. Her thrills come from being able to crinkle, punch, rip, or shake an object. The baby never realizes that the object is unique and capable of new reactions if it is handled in the right way.

The idea behind this activity is to see if the baby can open up her thinking and become more receptive to new ideas. Applying old ideas to objects isn't always bad. You'll see in Activity 69 how such thinking leads to imaginary play or pretending.

DIARY

_____

_____

_____

_____

_____

_____

_____

_____

GUIDE

The problem facing your baby is that she doesn't see the uniqueness of things. According to this cocky view, everything fits into one pattern, so why search for novelty?

One way to jolt this view is by presenting a toy which appears old but which actually is new. Put two old toys together in a new combination: For example, attach a bell to her rubber duck. Normally, the pattern for producing a noise with the bell is shaking, while the pattern for the duck is squeezing. But now a noise can be produced from the duck by shaking. Does your baby recognize that the old pattern is not holding? If so, what are her reactions? Does she take any time to examine the toy?

36. SPECIAL PLACES

Erik must have known he was fated to be a middle child. Anticipating a nosey big brother and a destructive little sister, he started preparing by finding special places for his playthings.

Earlier, he would indiscriminately drop a toy once he was finished with it. However, now having gained an understanding of space, the baby realizes that definite places exist for certain things. So, the baby deliberately puts toys in specific places and then he returns to those places whenever he wants to resume playing. Such actions were quite impossible a few weeks ago.

Regardless of how many children you have, it's always a good idea to give them a specially marked or colored bin, drawer, or box for keeping their personal or private things. At this point, your baby will appreciate such a gesture.

While he's finding places for toys, your baby is also searching for his place. Often the baby will challenge you to see just how far he can go before being considered out of place. For example, if you are trying to clean his bottle, your baby may refuse to give it up, menacingly shaking his head, "No!" You should realize that he's trying to establish his limits: Don't be too harsh with him.

Hand your baby a block, then shake a rattle. Does he release the block? Does he just drop it or does he find a special place for it? Remove the rattle. Does he immediately return to the block? Does he search for the block in a casual manner, as if he knew its exact location? Or is his search more frenzied?

While playing with your baby, keep in mind that you're trying to determine whether he understands that objects occupy definite places or spaces. This understanding of space is used ingeniously to overcome barriers in Activity 49.

DIARY

_____

_____

_____

_____

_____

GUIDE

Returning an object to a hiding place signifies that your baby is forming an understanding of space. To test the limits of this understanding, push the block slightly away from its original hiding place. Now, does he search for the toy casually or chaotically?

37. SPREAD-EAGLE

It used to be at bedtime that, once tucked in, Erin would sleep virtually in the same spot until morning. Now she's a nocturnal nomad, roaming up and down the sheets in search of a new place every night. As a result, you may often find her crunched up in a corner, spread-eagled in the center of the mattress, or with her arms and legs dangling out of the crib. With your baby really scooting around like this, it's wise to have bumper pads on the crib.

What's behind these bizarre postures? The baby probably has seen a toy she wants on a nearby windowsill or dresser, so she squirms and jockeys around until her legs and arms are lined up with the toy. She is convinced that once she's in the right position, she need only kick and wave, and the toy will be hers. Such reasoning stems from the earlier idea of space—that there's an exact place for everything. Unfortunately, your baby takes this concept and applies it to far space, that is, to an object that's out of reach. It never dawns on her that she must directly strike or hit an object in order to cause it to move. Simply getting in the right position and waving does not work for distant objects. Yet the baby persists until overcome by sleep. And that's why she's found the next morning slumped over in some exotic position.

Hold a stuffed animal over your baby's head. Does she stare at it? Does she squirm around? Watch her concern over making sure her head, arms, and legs are in the right position. Hang different toys above her, some near her stomach and chest, others to the right and left. Do you observe the same ritual? Is there ever waving or bouncing before your baby sets herself up into position?

At this point, your baby believes that she has to be a certain place before an object can be gained. Later, in Activity 61, she'll realize that her hands must move through space and contact objects in order to influence them.

DIARY

_____

_____

_____

_____

_____

_____

_____

_____

_____

GUIDE

To help your baby realize that contact with the toy is necessary, attach a long cord to a rattle. Then hold the toy high over your baby's head with the cord draping down on her hand. As your baby gets into position, she'll strike the cord, thus causing the toy to rattle. Striking the cord will make it easier for your baby to see the connection between contact and causality.

38. THE JUMP SEAT

Have you ever seen an infant jump seat? Supposedly it is so called because of its propulsion system—the baby's jumping and bouncing. Well, in Christopher's case, the name really came from the fact that if you didn't want to be tripped, rammed, or pinned to the wall, you learned to jump. Under Christopher's command, the seat was a liability. I still have the bruises to prove it. Many a night I vowed to trample it, and I would have if the seat had not been so well suited for Christopher's needs.

It was not that he needed to maim us; but he did have a need to discover outer space. Up until now, all of the baby's development had been geared to near space, that is, anything within reach. His dealings in near space were pretty advanced: He was learning a variety of ways to manipulate, handle, and use different objects. But what good was all this with objects that were out of reach, or in far space?

In desperation, the baby resorts to his earlier forms of wild arm-waving, kicking, and bouncing. If anything, these are effective in moving the jump seat closer to objects (to say nothing of drawing your attention), as well as causing an untold number of things to be accidentally hit, shoved, and made to fall through such outbursts.

If he were cocky before, now your baby is drunk with arrogance. Like a symphony conductor, he feels the world will jump out and respond to his wild arm-waving and bouncing. There's nothing he can't do; at least, that's his perception of the situation.

If you hold a rattle way above him, what does he do? Simply stare or look surprised? Do his arms beat like wings? Does his whole body shake like a bronco? How about his legs, are they kicking?

What's demonstrated by this frenetic play is that your baby has transferred his *magical thinking* from objects he can touch, like a rattle, to toys that are out of reach. These wild actions are a classic case of the child's Stage 3 magical thinking as it is now applied to objects in far space.

DIARY

_____

_____

_____

_____

_____

_____

_____

GUIDE

If your baby is completely stymied by things out of reach, see how he deals with another aspect of far space depth. Brush a doll across his hand and then drop it to the floor. Can he at least follow the toy to the floor with his eyes?

39. TOE SUCKING

It was amazing. One afternoon I popped into Christopher's room, and there he was sucking his toes. It was as if his legs were made of rubber. He could do anything with them, even drive you crazy. For this is also the time that the baby can effortlessly pull off his socks or bootees—after you have just spent ten minutes wrestling with him to get them on.

What's happening is that he is discovering his feet. During the last stage the baby was all wrapped up in his hands, learning prehension. But now, with all this bouncing and kicking, your baby is coming out with some pretty fancy footwork, at least good enough to gather in objects that would otherwise be out of reach.

Dangle a rattle over your baby's feet and make it brush his toes a few times. Does he raise his leg towards the rattle? Does he try to kick the toy? Move the rattle a little higher. Does he extend his leg? Raise the toy higher. Does he stretch for it or does he kick it into action?

If your baby stretches his leg, this shows that he's beginning to realize that he can get closer to, if not make contact with, the toy. In Activity 59, he will finally understand that leg contact is necessary if objects are to be controlled or affected in any way. Even if the child realized earlier that his hands needed to make contact, he does not automatically extend this understanding to his feet.

DIARY

_____

_____

_____

_____

_____

_____

_____

GUIDE

For the baby who easily extends his leg to keep up with the rattle, the following should present more of a challenge. Sweep the rattle to the right and then to the left. Can he move his legs sideways and track the toy?

40. STANDING UP

Around the end of this stage, one of the funniest things I encountered was Erin clutching a set of curtains and hoisting herself up to a standing position. Then, unable to let herself down, she panicked and screamed. Excited by her ability to stand, Erin continued this pulling up on furniture and getting stuck for a couple days. Then, one morning, instead of grabbing the table, Erin mistakenly yanked the tablecloth, sending our breakfast crashing to the floor.

Though I no longer considered it funny, I began to see some merit in the baby's actions, for now she would continually yank, reel in, and pull tablecloths, bed spreads, and even newspapers from my lap.

What started out as an activity for helping her stand now had an additional purpose: By yanking and pulling on tablecloths and spreads, Erin had discovered a means of bringing distant objects that were on the table or bed closer to herself. In short, she was bridging the gap to far space.

Many things, such as aspirin, creams, and sprays, that were once placed on tables or shelves and considered out of reach are now within easy grasp. You should become very conscious of this. But, as much as this is a time to be cautious, it's also a time to help your baby develop, as is suggested by the following activity.

Attach a long strand of yarn to a rattle, then hold and shake the toy as the end of the yarn rests on your baby's hand. After a few moments, does she pull on the yarn? Snip the yarn. Does she notice the release of the tension? Does she observe the falling yarn? Does she continue to yank on the flaccid yarn? Does she wave and kick?

This activity is undertaken to learn if your baby sees the connection between her hand and the strand of yarn. Your baby is learning to use things other than her hands as means to different ends. Activity 57 will soon show you how much progress she's made in this endeavor.

DIARY

_____

_____

_____

_____

_____

_____

_____

GUIDE

Snipping the yarn may be a little too advanced for the baby. Since she is still holding the yarn, it may never occur to her to look up and see if it is still connected to the rattle.

One step easier than the snipping is to slip the cord out of her hand as she tugs on it. Without the cord, what does your baby do? Does she stop tugging? If so, this indicates that your baby understands that the connection has been severed. But if tugging continues, this shows that your baby still believes that it's her hand and not the cord that causes the toy to move. She sees the cord only as a slightly more efficient means for causing the rattling.

41. DRUMMING

Around this time, most babies begin to have a thing for drums. You don't have to buy anything fancy; a ladle and pot will do. Erin used a spoon and would sit for fifteen to twenty minutes in front of a radiator, turning it into a xylophone.

The noise can drive you bananas, but there is some consolation in knowing that all this drumming means that your baby is making the connection between contact and causality: She now understands that contact must be made with the object if it is to produce sounds or if it is to be moved.

Hold a doll over your baby's head; then supply her with a little toothbrush or a spoon. Does she try to bat the doll? Does she swing the bat deliberately, with a purpose? Or does she just madly whip it around? Often you may have to brush the doll against the bat before your baby sees the connection between the two. Was this necessary with your baby?

The baby will use the toothbrush as a means only after she sees you doing it. At this point, she will not spontaneously pick up the brush and hit the toy.

DIARY

_____

_____

_____

_____

_____

_____

_____

GUIDE

Try swinging the rattle. Does she chase after it with the bat? This would indicate that your baby has given up the idea that there's such a thing as the "right position"; now she will change positions in order to make contact.

42. CUP-BANGING

Just like a scene out of a prison mess hall, there was Christopher sitting in his little high chair banging and rapping his cup.

Christopher had switched from the bottle to the cup pretty early. Occasionally, there had been spills and accidents, but nothing like this pounding. We were puzzled until a certain pattern in this banging emerged. From a dull methodical thud, the banging built up to unbelievably fast piston-like crashes. Christopher had discovered that different contacts caused different effects. By gradually increasing these intensities, as a scientist manipulates variables, our baby was performing a controlled experiment.

See if your baby will experiment. Supply him with a spoon, toothbrush, or comb. Next, as you hold it by its shoe lace, dangle a baby shoe over him. Does he concentrate on the shoe: Is the bat raised deliberately or swung wildly? Is the intensity increased or decreased? When he hits the shoe, does your baby start bouncing all around? Does he first try to bunt the shoe and then follow this with a slam?

Now the baby is beginning to test the relationship between the intensities of different swings. Hard swings produce different effects than soft swings. This understanding of intensity is really refined in Activity 54.

DIARY

_____

_____

_____

_____

_____

_____

GUIDE

The concept of varying intensities eventually becomes totally absorbed by your baby to the extent that it's even used in his magical thinking. Swing the shoe without giving him a bat. Does your baby shake and bounce? Does this shaking keep pace with the shoe? As the shoe loses momentum, does your baby slow down? Here is a case where your baby sees a relationship between the speed of an object and that of his gyrations, and he feels that the variations of his body movement are affecting the swing of the shoe.

43. BABIES AND PUPPIES

Ruppert was our first and biggest baby. The fact that he was a 200 pound St. Bernard made no difference to anyone, especially Christopher, who greeted the dog as he would any of us, with waves, giggles, and laughs. Then, almost overnight, a change developed. Now, when Ruppert lumbered by, Christopher would momentarily glance up and make a small, clawing gesture with his hand. Soon similar gestures were directed at us as well as to some of our son's favorite toys.

For example, if, while he was playing with some blocks, Christopher saw a rattle, he would make a brief stab at the air and then instantly return to his blocks.

Since babies do not yet have spoken language, during this period they develop hand signals or a body language to show that they recognize different objects: The clawing is a shorthand version of the way Ruppert would normally be petted or stroked, while stabbing the air is an abbreviated form of shaking a rattle.

The baby produces these gestures only to show that he understands how to use the things he's just seen. In no way does he desire the objects. That's why Christopher immediately resumed his playing after making the gestures. In a sense, it's your baby's way of saying "Hello," and "I know and recognize you."

Such a body language is economic, efficient, and extremely important, for it serves the foundation upon which the baby builds his verbal language.

Let's examine some of this pre-verbal language. Does your baby greet all people with the same signs? Do the signs hinge on how your baby feels about a person?

Initially, the gestures may all look the same or appear to be a code that's hard to break. But if you zero in on your baby's gestures, it will be evident that he has a clear and definite system for representing different objects.

While your baby is busy playing with a toy, show him a ball out of reach. Does he stop playing? Does he briefly cup his hands as if he were holding the ball? Bounce the ball. Does he quickly flap his hand?

This activity illustrates that the child is trying to communicate. Your baby's becoming more social, which indicates that Stage 3 is approaching its end.

DIARY

_____

_____

_____

_____

_____

GUIDE

Does your baby make these small gestures because he realizes that the toy is too far away to be grabbed? Move the ball closer. Does he continue playing with the blocks and still make the small gesture? Or does he try to grab the ball?

44. A VISIT TO THE DOCTOR

It was time for Erin's monthly check-up. No sooner had we entered the doctor's office than she started bawling. Earlier, such panic was registered only on seeing the nurses, their needles, the dressing tables, or old Doctor Benfield. But now, merely being in the doctor's waiting room touched off these hysterics.

Needless to say, this behavior was frought with fear. However, on the intellectual side, it indicated that the baby was able to anticipate events: a sure sign of *symbolic thinking*. At this point, Erin needed only a few clues in order to put together a picture of what was soon to happen. Another example of this new thinking occurred when Erik screwed up his face on seeing either an approaching washcloth or a spoonful of mushy carrots.

Can your baby anticipate events? Try playing with her in the following manner: Approach your baby with a bib. Does she anticipate what will happen? Does she laugh or squeal? Does she dip her chin, elevate her shoulders, and crunch down her neck in anticipation? Next, pick out something the baby likes, such as a big terry cloth towel. If your baby is high-strung, she may over-anticipate, while a low-keyed child will be modest in her anticipations.

What we're seeing in this activity is that the baby's present behavior is influenced by her past experiences. Later, as shown in Activity 66, the baby will anticipate certain things without having had any prior experiences with them.

DIARY

_____

_____

_____

_____

_____

_____

GUIDE

Some babies may not exhibit anticipation if they are only waiting to have something done to them, like a bib tucked in or their face cleaned. On the other hand, if the object closing in signals that your baby will be doing something, then the anticipation should surface. Slowly bring towards your baby a cup or pot with a lid that can be directly manipulated. Does this trigger off the anticipation?

45. SOOOOO BIG

"How big are you? Sooooo big?" This was Erik's favorite game. Like a giant bird stretching out its wings, Erik was spreading out his arms in response to my, "How big are you?"

Obviously the appeal of this game is that your baby is playing with you and not with some stuffed animal. Also, it is a form of play that's perfectly matched to your baby's latest level of cognitive functioning. The big sweeping arm motions found in "Sooooo Big" are the very same actions your baby has just developed as a means for signaling you to continue whatever you've been doing.

If you are shaking a rattle, he will remain entranced until you stop. Then, with exaggerated and commanding waves, you are signaled to reshake the toy. Not to be confused with those earlier thrashings, the present big waves are more orderly and involve only the specific parts of the body required for operating the toy.

Wind up a music box. When it slows down, what does your baby do? Try to grab it? Bang another toy? Shake all over? Or command, with big motions, to start winding? If you are slow to respond, what does he do? Start his magical routine? Or simply wait? The latter shows that the baby is losing faith in his magical actions and is beginning to concede that something hinges on you.

These exaggerated gestures are the baby's way of telling you that he wants something to continue. When the baby eventually gets to Activity 58, you'll be able to observe how much more sophisticated he's become in getting you to work for him.

DIARY

_____

_____

_____

_____

_____

_____

_____

GUIDE

There are times when your baby has to be playing directly with something before the big movements begin. Take a paper cup with a lid. As your baby watches, remove the lid and snap it back on. Do this a few times and then hand him the cup with the lid still on. After trying to pry off the lid, does the baby offer you the cup? Or does he make those exaggerated hand movements?

46. THE BRONX CHEER

Christopher's sole accomplishment, as far as utterances go, was the Bronx cheer. It drove his grandmothers to distraction. While baby cousins and nephews were blowing kisses, babbling vowels, and occasionally even saying "Ma-Ma" and "Da-Da," Christopher reveled in blowing out his cheer. He did make one concession by imitating their "Bye-Bye" waves; but could rarely resist punctuating the waves with a rousing cheer.

What escaped most of us was that the cheering and waving mirrored a significant intellectual development. Earlier, Christopher had been limited to imitating only actions that he already possessed: It was easy for him to copy you blowing bubbles or making a fist but he could not repeat your sounds nor could he perform any intricate hand-waving. Now he could imitate most new behaviors just as long as they were simple and could be seen or heard.

Make sure you don't pressure your kids to get them to do new things just because other children are doing them. Imitation is a unique ability. Some babies have it but won't perform while others are slow to pick it up. Whatever the case, never force your baby to imitate.

Of the following, which can your baby imitate: Clapping his hands? Rubbing his hands? Making a fist and then raising his thumb? Can your baby imitate animal sounds (barking, meowing, etc.)? If you hit two toys together, can your baby copy you? What sounds are easiest for your baby to copy? What about noises made by objects such as a hissing kettle or a squeaky wheel? Can your baby imitate these sounds?

The purpose of this play is to learn about your baby's ability to imitate. During this stage, his imitations are limited to rather simple behaviors involving parts of his body he can see. Within a few months, as you will see in Activity 67, your baby will be able to copy a range of very intricate and subtle behaviors.

DIARY

_____

_____

_____

_____

_____

_____

_____

_____

GUIDE

A real test for your baby is to imitate actions that are partially obscured from his vision, such as opening his mouth, sticking out his tongue, yawning, or sucking a finger. Can your baby imitate any of these acts?

47. POP GOES THE WEASEL

If Erik's favorite amusement was "Sooooo Big," Erin's was "Pop Goes the Weasel." She loved the onomatopoeia and would often repeat some explosive sounds like "Po-Po-Po." Such nursery rhymes were truly helping her language evolve. After listening to them often, she would chant a chorus of syllables. However, Erin's most spectacular verbal exhibition consisted of rants and raves expressed in a steady jumble of babbles, sounds, grunts, groans, syllables, and near-words that, if copied down, would have filled the pages of a notebook.

In addition to being able to express so much, Erin was gaining a wide range of comprehension. For example, she understood "No!" She also realized that some places were off limits and that certain acts were always prohibited. It was not only the tone of your voice; she definitely associated the word with certain things. I can remember her crawling to the toilet, turning to check me out, and then plunging her hands into the bowl, knowing darn well that this was a "No-No." On anticipating our reaction, she would make a beeline to an open door, knowing a "No!" would be coming but trying to outrace it.

At this point, you are going to find that, progressively, more of the syllables your baby utters are those that are contained in words familiar to her.

Try sounding out her name. Can she say the syllables? Of the syllables she uses, which are the clearest and most distinct? If your baby says a clear syllable like "Ba" and you tag on "Be," will she repeat the polysyllable "Ba-Be?" What sounds will she mimic? Will your baby repeat "Ma-Ma" and "Da-Da?"

Your baby is laying the foundation for speech with her syllables. In Activity 68, she will string these syllables together into words.

DIARY

_____

_____

_____

_____

_____

GUIDE

Often, it's easier for your baby to say sounds when the objects or toys referred to are in front of her. Hold up the rattle and call out its name. Does she try to copy you?

48. PEEK-A-BOO

Like most babies, ours could never resist peek-a-boo. Sinking and then bobbing up from behind the crib drove our kids into gales of laughter. The popularity of this game rests on a new intellectual concept called _object permanence._ Such a concept entails a fresh understanding of space, time, and the properties of objects. Before, when a person or toy disappeared, the baby assumed that it no longer existed. But now she realizes that something can temporarily vanish, and yet still exist.

Being able to tolerate your brief disappearances is another level of trust that will continue to build up over the next few months.

But don't hide too long. If you fail to pop up within a certain interval, your baby may grow nervous or she may even just turn away, preferring to believe, as she once did, that you no longer exist. Timing is very important. It is just one of the clues your baby relies on to help her understand this new concept. Another clue is using parts to identify a whole. Earlier, a partially hidden toy would never be recognized; now it can be.

Using a handkerchief, cover a doll so that only its legs show. Does your baby pick it right up? Next have only its feet showing. Will she

still pick it up? Now cover it all up, but make sure the doll's silhouette is outlined on the handkerchief. Can your baby still recognize the doll?

This play reveals that your baby understands the fundamentals of *object concept*, that is, the realization that an object exists even though it can't be seen. If a toy disappears, she searches for it. Before, she would consider that the missing toy had ceased to exist. In Activities 60, 61, 62, and 63, you will soon be able to record how much progress your baby has made with this concept.

DIARY

_____

_____

_____

_____

_____

_____

_____

GUIDE

The most difficult accomplishment for your baby is to recognize a toy when its outline is not shown. Put a rattle beneath a box. Will your baby look under the box? Shake the rattle while it's covered. Does this help her know to pick up the box?

DEVELOPING
TOOLS

Eight to Fourteen Months

Your baby bursts into this stage with a fantastic urge to feel and explore every little toy around him. But he is stopped because many of these toys are either blocked, out of reach, or hidden from him. So he spends the next six months working on behaviors or tools to help him overcome these obstacles.

At first your baby is terribly awkward when it comes to getting around barriers. For example, something as simple as a toy blocked by a pillow leads him to kick his feet, to shake his head, and to jab aimlessly at the air as if this magical ritual would remove the barrier. Some babies are challenged by such a barrier, while others fall apart with frustration when they try to get through to the toy. Regardless of the reaction, babies now begin to exhibit a greater awareness of their own limitations. Hence they buckle down, become more conservative, and begin to rely on you for an awful lot of things.

Steadily, your baby tries to develop his hands into fine, precise, and sensitive tools. This new sensitivity leads to the discovery that all toys are unique, differing in size, shape, weight, texture, and so on. No longer does your baby treat all toys in the same way. Now your baby realizes that each has its own nature and is independent of his actions. In a sense, he considers toys as having minds of their own. This recognition applies not only to toys but also to people. For the first time, it hits him, that we can come and go independently of his wishes. This is why he cries when you start to move away: He knows that you are going and that he cannot stop you.

It is interesting that, around this time, your baby's behavior becomes so precise that she can copy most of your little quirks and actions. It is as if she feels that by imitating you she can preserve your presence even when you aren't there.

Gradually, your baby's mind develops to a point that it can generate some sophisticated behaviors. For instance, the baby's able to find hidden objects; to anticipate someone's departure; and to remove barriers, all of which require an understanding of basic concepts involving space, time, distance, and cause and effect. Such concepts form the foundation for the thinking processes used by adults to solve scientific, logical, and mathematical problems.

As her thinking progresses, your baby becomes far less dependent upon you. Perhaps the clearest example of this new independence can be seen in her legs. She can stand alone and is now capable of using her feet to kick closer to herself toys that are beyond the reach of her hand. In the past, she needed you to get these objects and to help her stand. But as this stage evolves, she becomes more capable of doing these and other things on her own.

However, your baby doesn't completely break from you. If anything, a partnership is formed. She does her part and isn't totally dependent upon you, but she realizes when she should call you in. As a result of this new arrangement, your baby is becoming more willing to cooperate and to make compromises, which is a far cry from the self-centered egotism of Stage Three.

In summary, your baby moves through three phases during the "Tool Stage": from (1) the clumsy phase in which he cannot remove barriers and is dependent on you, to (2) the transition phase in which his *tools,* such as kicking, are sufficiently well-developed to enable him to strike out on his own, and finally to (3) the partnership phase in which his tools are developed as well as they're going to be and he knows when to call on you and when to rely on himself.

Let's now turn to the activities and see just what your baby is doing in the "Tool Stage."

49. TIGHT SPACES

I was home one afternoon with Christopher, and as he began to amuse himself, I drifted away, hoping to finish some work of my own. I must have been preoccupied for at least twenty minutes when it suddenly dawned on me that I had seen neither hide nor hair of our baby. Casually, I called and started searching for him. But when he was nowhere to be found, I desperately raced from room to room until my tension reached a point of near panic, whereupon, out of nervous exhaustion, I pitched myself onto the couch. As I sunk down through the cushions like a dead weight, I heard a thud accompanied by a "Na-Na." It was Christopher. He had wormed his way under the couch and had been there all this time.

After pulling myself together, my first thoughts were that taking care of a baby is a full-time job. Admittedly, there are other things that must be done at home, but your baby has to come first. Organize your work so you can make periodic checks on the baby. At this time, with all his crawling and moving around, you may want to fasten little bells to his shirt so his whereabouts can be monitored.

In addition to crawling, your baby is also capable of slithering and wiggling through tight spaces such as those under couches or between chairs. Earlier, such pieces of furniture represented obstacles, but now Christopher has learned to adapt in order to overcome these barriers.

Intellectually and emotionally, your baby realizes that he must change to meet the requirements of the world around him. No longer is he cocky and self-centered.

To get an idea of how well your baby can adapt to barriers, try the following: Partially hide a block behind a balloon. Does he try to squeeze under or go over the barrier? Does he push or pull it? Does he attack it by striking out at it? Or does he fall back on his wild arm-waving and body-rocking?

Here your baby is beginning to use his hands as means or tools for adapting to his environment. Later, the use of means will have developed to a very complex level, as illustrated by Activity 79.

DIARY

_____

_____

_____

_____

_____

GUIDE

If your baby uses his magical arm waving, this means that he is still in the previous stage. To help him catch up, maneuver the balloon in front of his flailing arms so that it will accidently be knocked away. Repeated experiences like this may give him the idea that he has to hit the balloon, and that aimless arm-waving is futile.

50. A BULL IN A CHINA SHOP

Erik was the type of baby who had to eat in isolation because if there were anything around—cups, saucers, or bowls—he would surely bull right through them. Just the other morning he spied an orange behind an empty glass and instead of reaching around the glass he merely extended his arm and knocked over the glass as if it weren't there. In reality, the glass didn't exist for Erik because he had not yet discovered the concept of transparency. As long as he can see through something, be it a glass or window, it's not considered a barrier.

During this period, for our sanity and Erik's safety, we found it was best to set the table with brightly colored paper cups instead of clear plastic tumblers.

Just as your baby needs well-marked barriers, she also seeks well-defined limits. She realizes how dependent she is upon you and awaits your help and guidance. This is the time when she learns to obey your "Nos" and willingly responds to such requests as, "Open your mouth," "Come here!" and "Bring me the doll."

In the preceding activity you observed your baby attempting to overcome the balloon barrier. This was an easy task since the balloon was somewhat transparent.

Let's see how your baby handles a hard barrier, one that's not transparent. Take a pillow, and partially hide a toy behind it. How does she remove the pillow? Is it different from the way she removed the balloon?

While playing in this manner, your baby is learning the basics about time: First she must remove the pillow before she can have the toy. In Activity 99, you'll be able to observe how much your baby's understanding of time has developed.

DIARY

_____

_____

_____

_____

_____

_____

GUIDE

Quickly brush your baby's hand with the toy, and then partially hide the toy again behind the pillow. Such brushing puts her in touch with the toy. She may need this extra contact because the pillow allows so little of the toy to be seen.

51. A TUG OF WAR

Erin had developed a new game of constantly giving you objects and then taking them back. After she handed me a little doll, I tucked it under my arm and proceeded to read the morning paper. In a moment, she was back and started to yank and tug the doll from under my arm. Never once did she try to lift my arm.

At this point your baby has come to rely upon you so much that she only sees such things as balloons and pillows as barriers. But your hands are not a barrier; she puts them in the same category as her hands: helpful tools for overcoming obstacles. That's why, if you grab a toy that your baby's playing with, she might look surprised, puzzled, or annoyed. But she won't strike away your hand; your baby will merely pull on the toy as though she's having a tug of war.

Try grabbing a toy that your baby's playing with. Does she start a tug of war? Does she look at your hand at all? Does she seem surprised, puzzled, or annoyed?

With this play, you can see that your baby still hasn't properly classified your hands. Shortly she'll be able to perform this classification, as is shown in Activity 55.

DIARY

_____

_____

_____

_____

_____

GUIDE

When she tugs on the toy, really shake and wiggle it. This may give her the idea that your hand is an obstacle.

52. NUDITY

Erik had a new trick. But we knew whenever he had pulled it off, because he would imperiously bellow to be taken out of his crib. Arriving in his room, we would be presented with a little boy prancing around in his crib completely nude. Erik had learned to take off his pants and diaper.

Don't get upset over your baby's nudity, even in public. His actions are not intended to be lewd. However, if you treat his nudity as a problem, your child may soon acquire all kinds of distorted notions about his body.

Remember, try to look at your baby's action from his point of view rather than your own. In this case, Erik's ability to take off his pants and diaper signals that he's now capable of removing two barriers.

Being able to handle two barriers signals a new cognitive development.

As babies rely more and more on thinking and planning out their actions, they begin to look for logical outcomes. For example, once they knock away a pillow, they expect a toy to be freely theirs. When, instead, they meet another barrier, several reactions are possible. Some babies get all the more fired up and see this as a challenge; others pause and rethink the situation; while some bear down and plod on. These various reactions show how behavior is a blend of intelligence and personality.

To see how your baby reacts to a double barrier, try the following: Set a pillow up like a screen between you and your baby; hold the toy in your hand, hiding it partially behind the pillow. Once he breaks past the pillow and grabs the toy you're holding, a tug of war will start. After a few moments, give up the toy.

Being able to handle two barriers is a good example of a Stage 4 achievement. Now your baby is really making his hands work for him instead of just waving and shaking them, as was the case in Stage 3 whenever he encountered a complex problem.

DIARY

GUIDE

Since this activity hinges on his personality, use a toy your baby really likes or a new one that will spark his interest.

53. LIGHT BULBS AND SOCKETS

For exploring new objects, Erin has developed a special tool, her finger. She pokes it into everything. Wielding such a tool in this manner can be dangerous, especially around empty light sockets and exposed outlets. Make sure, from here on in, that all light sockets are filled and that electrical outlets are taped over.

However, no matter how cautious you are, the baby will find something to poke. For example, while visiting her aunt, Erin noticed a beautifully sculptured jello salad shimmering on the kitchen table. In a flash, her fingers had torpedoed the jello, leaving it with a big sagging hole in its side. Immediately Erin drew back, realizing that she had done something wrong.

Your baby is beginning to recognize that not all objects can be poked; some are different and require different handling. This realization is especially clear when it comes to dealing with barriers. Now your baby will pause and "size up" a barrier rather than keep hitting it. The only drawback with this is that the "sizing up" always comes too late: She thinks of it only after her attacks on the barrier have failed.

Take a toy and cover a quarter of it with a new or unusual barrier, such as a book. Does she stop and size up the barrier after she has hit it a few times?

At this point, your baby is beginning to accommodate or match her behavior to the object she's playing with. By the time Activity 64 is reached, accommodation will be operating on an even more advanced level.

DIARY

_____

_____

_____

_____

_____

_____

_____

GUIDE

Try books of different shapes and weights. If a heavy book follows a light one, the difference should make your baby pause and size things up.

54. FINGER PAINTING

All of a sudden Christopher wants to paint, but not with a brush or paper. Instead, using his fingers as a brush, he dabbles in strained carrots, oatmeal, and chocolate pudding.

As you can imagine, such artistry can stir up a lot of commotion during meals. However, I find myself not snapping at Christopher but rather, I am more inclined to form a partnership within which both our needs can be met. For instance, now I provide our baby with exotically patterned placemats that are far more interesting to finger and trace than are his bland carrots.

My willingness to bend and compromise is exceeded only by Christopher's. It seems, during this stage, that your baby realizes how much of what he wants to do hinges on you. This is a far cry from the self-centeredness of Stage 3. For the first time, your baby is beginning to recognize how interwoven and interdependent everything is.

Such thinking also applies to barriers. No longer does Christopher beat them as hard as he used to. If anything, they are handled with care, gently nudged, picked up, or slid away. Why the change of heart? Because now our boy understands that if he strikes too hard, the toy behind the barrier may be knocked out of reach. This new behavior is a strong sign that his reasoning has gone beyond simple cause and effect thinking. He now sees his acts as a chain reaction, involving many causes and effects: A hand strike knocks away the pillow which, in turn, may knock the toy our of reach.

Go back and set up some of the toys and barriers that you have already used and see how he treats the barriers now. Does he hold back his striking?

With this play, your baby is learning some nuances about cause and effect. The slightest change in a variable can cause different effects. Eventually this understanding will be applied to some sophisticated tower building, as shown in Activity 76.

DIARY

_____

_____

_____

_____

_____

_____

GUIDE

As you have done before, set up a pillow with a block behind it. But this time, place it near the edge of your lap or of a table, so that if your baby strikes too hard, the toy will fall to the floor. Doing this a number of times may make your baby change his way of handling barriers.

If this or any other activity bothers him, frustrates him, or makes him cry, then stop what you are doing. During an advanced part of the "Tool Stage," knocking toys to the floor will amuse him.

55. THE BABY SITTER

Around this time, Erik would get upset when left with a baby sitter. Then we found Jackie, who could play, for an entire afternoon, our little boy's favorite game—patty-cake. Erik loved to push your hands back and forth and even spar with you. It took Jackie only a few minutes to find this out. We were lucky with Jackie; such baby sitters are hard to find.

I've never been able to fathom why we're so selective when it comes to finding someone to fix our hair or our car, when we are almost indifferent about whom we allow to care for our baby. Why is it that we don't trust an amateur with our hair or our car yet we are willing to trust an untested fourteen year old with our baby?

Our practice for selecting baby sitters is as follows. Call those who are recommended highly by parents whose views on child care are similar to your own. Invite the sitter fifteen minutes early so you can observe her handling your baby. Does she interact with the baby? Does she ask questions such as: "What's his favorite toy?" "Has he eaten?" "How old is he?" "Does he like to be read to?" If this information is not requested, then write it out—along with the telephone numbers of your doctor, neighbors, relatives, and where you can be reached in case of an emergency.

A book like *Help Your Baby Learn,* especially with its Diary section laced with personal comments about your baby's growth, development, personality, likes and dislikes, would be instructive reading for a baby sitter. She would learn that patty-cake signals that your baby is about to make a big intellectual leap: He's going to start using your hands to get toys that are out of reach. Here's what you should be looking for.

Notice when your baby first starts playing with your hands. Earlier in this stage, he either treated them like his own hands or just ignored them. But now he feels that, with some hard work, they can be shaped into useful tools for his purposes. So he starts to work on them.

If you are both holding a toy, rather than starting a tug of war, he now puts down his end of the toy and begins to peel your fingers off the other end.

Shortly he will be able to do two things at once: He will hold one end of the toy while peeling your fingers off the toy with his other hand. Intellectually, this is real progress. It shows that he can keep his mind on two things at once: Holding the toy and attempting to remove your fingers.

Finally, he becomes so confident that he no longer peels away your fingers, but merely pushes your hand off the toy. As far as he is concerned, you're tamed and under his command. He will even play patty-cake and spar with you.

To see how far he is into this phase, hand your baby a clothespin, a paper roll or some kind of tube that he can easily hold. Now hold on to it. Does he drop the tube and peel your fingers away from it? Does he hold the tube and peel your fingers away from it? Or does he push your hand off?

The baby now realizes that your hands, as well as his own, can be used as means to an end.

In Activity 86, your baby's thinking develops to the point where it can invent such means symbolically.

DIARY

_____

_____

_____

_____

_____

_____

_____

_____

GUIDE

Hold the tube with your left hand and use your right to jab at your baby's attacking hand. This may challenge or push him to the point where he almost rips your hand from the tube as a way of showing that he is in full command.

56. BANGING TOYS

With Christopher, there was never a dull moment. Neither was there ever a silent moment. He had always made noise, but during this stage it was deafening, for he would slam blocks together as if they were cymbals. Although now Christopher has some control of my hands, he has little control over his own. For example, he can't even drop a toy out of one hand to pick up a second. What happens is that he picks up the second toy so that he has one in each hand. But he really doesn't want this. What he desires is to put both hands around the second toy. However, since he can't drop the first toy, he ends up banging both toys together.

The manner in which your baby deals with this situation will tell you something about his personality. He may find the banging so hilarious that he gets carried away, and in the process one of the toys may accidently slip out of his hands. Or he may get so frustrated that his ranting and raving lead to dropping a toy. Regardless of his temperament, your baby can't deliberately put one toy down and pick up another.

While he is playing with a block, hand him a small ball. What happens? Does he bang the ball and block together? Does he think it's funny?

Remember that this activity shows some pretty complex thinking. The mind is trying to coordinate simultaneously two competing ideas: holding on with one hand and letting go with the other.

DIARY

_____

_____

_____

_____

_____

GUIDE

Make the first toy a big one, such as a ball, balloon, or teddy bear, so that he has to hold it with two hands. When you offer him the second toy, he will reach out for it and the big one will drop. This may start him thinking about dropping toys intentionally.

57. THE PIGGY-BACK

As I sat on the couch, Erik pulled himself up, crawled over, and started pushing my shoulder. He was trying to get me to give him a piggy-back ride.

Asking for a piggy-back ride is a clear illustration of your baby's changing attitude towards you. Now you're pictured as a helper who can literally support or boost along your baby's development. Earlier, you were either ignored or considered an obstacle. But at this point you're seen by your baby as an extension of herself. By working with you, she can succeed; alone she would fail.

As she grows older, this idea of working with others will serve as the basis for her participation in groups and other social organizations. For now, though, this thinking helps her understand her limits as well as your powers.

If a toy is too high, she will push your hand towards it. Your baby does this with such ease because she now can calculate distances mentally. She knows in advance whether she can or cannot reach the toy. This cuts down all unnecessary behaviors such as trying to grab the toy herself; your baby merely turns to you for help. In short, she is planning or thinking out her behaviors before she acts.

Earlier, her planning always came too late. She only thought about her acts after they had failed. There was little pre-planning or elimination of useless acts as there is now.

Sit next to something like a bookcase and place a bell on a high shelf so that it is out of your baby's reach. Does she automatically push your arm towards the bell? If she hasn't developed the use of your hand, she may just stare at the bell or lunge for it. She may even resort to her old "magic," such as shaking her hands and rocking her body. What *does* she do?

As this activity illustrates, your baby is using you more and more to adapt to her world. During this stage, your baby begins to realize how indispensable you are to her intellectual and emotional well-being.

DIARY

GUIDE

Your baby may not push your hand right away because she doesn't see the connection between it and the bell, so try raising your hand a few times and shaking the bell.

58. A RIDE IN THE CAR

Whenever Erin became bored and restless, we had the perfect stimulant—a ride in the car. She'd get so excited that before I could even strap her into her car seat, Erin would squirm away and start pulling, pushing, and banging all the knobs, buttons, and dials on the dashboard. However, when it came to the car's radio, she'd turn and start pulling, pushing, and grabbing my arm.

She'd found, from earlier experiences, that the radio was too difficult for her to switch on, so she was signaling me to do it. This indicated that Erin realized that my hands were something more than just a means to gather in objects that were out of reach. Now she perceived them as more competent than hers in dealing with objects that were within reach, such as the car's radio.

Wind up a little music box and put it next to your baby. When it stops, what does she do? Does she try to wind it herself? Does she simply stare at it? Does she use any of her wild arm waving? Or does she push your hand towards the box?

At this time, the baby is able to classify her hands as competent or incompetent. Later, in Activity 100, you'll see how such a classification can involve emotional turmoil.

DIARY

_____

_____

_____

_____

_____

GUIDE

Being able to understand that you make the music is a hard concept to grasp. So pretend to wind the box: Go through all the motions. Then, when it still doesn't play, your baby may get the idea and start pushing your hands.

59. KICKING

Since learning to stand, Christopher has hated to be off his feet, even to have a wet, soggy diaper changed. He'll kick, wiggle, and squirm until you stick either him or yourself with the diaper pin.

Putting a toy in Christopher's hand while he's being changed seems to distract him and make diapering easier.

As much as the kicking is a form of resistance, it's also the baby's way of showing his independence. Throughout this stage, most of the baby's experiences have pointed to his dependence on you. Now, with standing and kicking, he has finally found some things he can do without your help. In more ways than one, he's learning to stand on his own two feet.

A good example of the independence the baby has gained through his kicking can be seen in his ability to gather in with his feet toys that are beyond his reach. If there's a little rattle near his toe, he can guide it with his feet to his hands. As a result of this new behavior, he now spends less time working with your hands and more time using his feet.

Over the coming weeks, you will see more independent actions as your baby develops such behaviors as walking, climbing, talking, exploring, and the like. Such new behaviors are going to cause a lot of things to change; in particular the ways you play with him will change. Earlier, I suggested handing him toys if he pushed your hand towards them. This was matching your play with his level of development. But now he can do things on his own and doesn't need your hands.

Kicking is important because it alerts us to this change. It points to his coming independence and also to the fact that we must change our playing to suit his new level of development. In essence, he is "kicking the habit" of dependence.

Pick up a doll and stretch your arm so that you are holding it over your baby's feet. What happens? Does he push your hands? Does he wiggle his feet? Does he shake his body?

This kicking is a good example of how your baby now copes with objects that are out of reach or in far space. In Activity 81 you'll be able to record how much progress he's made in understanding space.

DIARY

_____

_____

_____

_____

_____

_____

_____

_____

GUIDE

If at first your baby doesn't kick, bounce the doll up and down on his toes.

60. ELVES, MIDGETS,
AND OTHER LITTLE PEOPLE

While most kids love to watch T.V., Erin loves to watch it go off. As soon as this happens, she scurries behind the set and peers through its perforated backing in what seems to be an attempt to catch a glimpse of the elves, midgets, and other tiny people as they're leaving the screen.

Apparently what she's thinking is that once the people are no longer on the screen they have to be somewhere; so she searches for them. This is pretty sophisticated reasoning. Earlier, if something disappeared, its existence was considered to have ceased, so your baby wouldn't bother searching for it. Now your baby will go after a hidden object, whether it's a T.V. character or a toy, because she realizes that such things still exist even if they can't be seen. What makes this kind of reasoning possible is that your baby can create images or symbolic pictures in her mind of things that have disappeared. The image of the character or toy is a constant reminder for her to search.

In Erin's case, we pushed the T.V. flush against the wall so she wouldn't be shocked, and then we began to play a searching game with her.

Try this game with your baby. While she's watching you, hide a toy under a little box. Does she have a blank look on her face, implying "What happened?" Or does your baby slowly pick up the box? Is she surprised to find the toy?

Here the baby is beginning to understand that if an object disappears, it must exist somewhere else. This understanding is known as *object concept*.

DIARY

_____

_____

_____

_____

_____

_____

_____

GUIDE

If your baby shows a blank expression, slowly picks up the box, or looks surprised at finding the toy, this means that she is still a little shaky when it comes to using symbols and images. To help her along, put the toy under a napkin and tuck it in so that the form of the toy is bulging beneath the napkin and outlined by it.

61. DADDY'S SHOES

Have you ever overslept and been late for an important meeting? And then, in the midst of gobbling down your breakfast and frantically trying to get dressed, you jam your toes into a shoe that's packed with an old gushy diaper!

Well, this is just a sample of what it's been like for the last few weeks—ever since Erin became totally fascinated with dropping her playthings into my shoes. Finally I got smart and lent Erin a pair of tattered sneakers, for which she's been eternally grateful.

Although I was exasperated at finding the diaper in my shoe, it did indicate that our baby was making progress in understanding *object permanence*. Until recently, her searching had been limited to objects that could be easily found or immediately grabbed. However, if a doll were hidden a little too far under a pillow so as to prevent immediate contact, then Erin would stop searching. The reason for this was that her image of the doll was still hazy and would fade unless she touched the toy right away. But now her images are more lasting and can guide a search for longer periods of time.

Searching for extended lengths of time demonstrates that your baby is developing persistence and self-discipline. Rather than always running to you for help, she's more inclined to work things out for herself. This persistence adds to your baby's growing sense of independence and self-sufficiency.

Let's see if your baby can persist and undertake an extended search. Drop a small toy down into the bottom of a sock. Will she stretch down for it? If she doesn't stretch for it, what does she do? Does she look surprised, lost, or bewildered?

This activity is a more in-depth probe to see how well your baby understands *object concept.* Later, in Activity 91, you'll be able to observe how much her thinking has advanced in this area.

DIARY

_____

_____

_____

_____

_____

_____

_____

_____

_____

GUIDE

Try dropping a drinking straw into the sock. The straw is long, so your baby won't have to stretch too far. Whenever she pulls out the straw, clip off a piece, making it a little shorter and thus requiring her to dig down a little deeper each time.

62. EATING ON THE RUN

Since he has learned to crawl, Erik's eating has really slumped. Now, our baby stuffs his mouth, yells to get out of his chair, and then in a moment is clamoring to be put back up to finish his toast.

Rather than continuing to pick him up, I thought it would be simpler to place the toast on the seat of his high chair where he could reach it easily. But this produced chaos. As far as Erik was concerned, the toast could only be on the tray of his high chair. Even when he saw me move it to the seat, he would always return to the tray. Then when he was shown the toast on the seat, our baby would act surprised. And surprised he was, for at this time a baby can't search in two places for an object. It's hard for him to create two images. It's as if your baby's mind only had enough "intellectual film" to take one picture or make one image. When he sees you first hiding a toy, he'll make an image of this. But if you then remove the toy and hide it in a different place, he can't create a second image showing this new hiding place. Without this second image, he doesn't have a guide, so he stops searching.

Try hiding a toy in two places. First put it under a little box, and while your baby is watching, take the toy out and put it under a napkin. Does he look under the napkin? Or does he go back to the box? If he picks up the box, what is his expression? Does he search anywhere else?

This activity shows the way in which your baby's understanding of *object concept* relies on his ability to use symbols. Eventually, in Activity 98, you'll be able to observe how sophisticated his symbolic thinking has become as it relates to object concept.

DIARY

_____

_____

_____

_____

_____

GUIDE

While the toy is under the napkin, give your baby a brief glimpse of it. This may give him enough time to create an image of the toy in its second hiding place.

63. THE VEST POCKET

Erik had a keen eye for detail. Whenever you were wearing something new, he was the first to notice and the first to touch it. Once, while he was stroking a new coat of mine, Erik found some keys in one of the pockets. Playfully, I grabbed the keys and dropped them into my pants' pocket. Without hesitation, he dove his hand into this pocket and came up with the keys. However, when, in plain view, I then slid the keys into my vest pocket, our little boy froze and stopped searching. Although he could find the keys when they were hidden in the coat and pants, he couldn't find them when they were hidden in a third place, the vest pocket. Our baby could only find an object if it had been hidden in no more than two places.

Intellectually, at this point, your baby can grasp the significance of two; any number beyond this is really incomprehensible.

Let's see how your baby can handle two or more hiding places. Set up two hiding places, a box and a napkin, and then use your shirt pocket for the third place. Now, in plain view, move the toy from the box to the napkin, and then to your pocket. He'll look under the napkin first and then go back to the box, without ever considering the pocket. It's as if the gears of his mind are locked between the box and the napkin. Even if you use only two places, the box and the pocket or the napkin and the pocket, it's still the same: Your baby will go only to the original hiding places, the box and the napkin.

While your baby follows your movements, try moving the toy from the box to the napkin to the pocket. What happens? Is he stuck with either the box or the napkin? What does he do when the toy isn't under either of his old hiding places?

As he plays in this fashion, your baby is experimenting with *object concept* and also applying his understanding of number. In Activity 88, he will further advance this understanding of number by working on problems involving seriation—the ability to put things in order by size.

DIARY

GUIDE

If your baby doesn't search in your pocket, try lifting his hand into it.

64. FAVORITE TOYS

It never ceases to amaze me that Christopher and Erik can be brothers and yet can still be so different in temperament. Christopher is a gadfly: always talking, tagging along, or having to be the center of things. Erik, in contrast, is content to sit back, listen, and take the feelings of others into consideration.

Trying to be fair, we started out by treating the boys the same, but it never worked out. Erik was easy; you had to tell him something just once. However, Christopher had to be dealt with more firmly. We constantly had to spell out what he could and could not do; otherwise he'd be up to his neck in trouble.

With Erik, we could bend the rules; with Christopher, they had to be followed to a "T." When he knew his limits, Christopher was great. He had a lot of fun; people could be nice to him; and he felt good about himself. The fairest way you could treat Christopher was to be firm. No single method works for all kids. Fairness is being able to act in a way that's most appropriate to the particular child.

Most of us can cope with big differences like temperament, but it's those little day-to-day things that really tax our patience and fairness. For example, whereas Erik took little stock in toys, Christopher would scream bloody murder if a favorite toy were moved, let alone missing. Even if the lost toy were replaced with an identical one, Christopher could immediately detect the substitute and would then yell that much louder.

During these times, it was hard to keep our cool until we noticed the method Christopher used to distinguish his favorite toy from a substitute. He would gently brush his hands over the toys. No longer were toys bluntly grabbed, twisted, and shaken. Rather, they were examined like jewels as he gently slid his fingers over their sides, poking and probing their tiniest cracks and scratches. Our baby was developing his hands into highly sensitive tools for discriminating.

By pawing over all these little details, Christopher could now tell the difference between toys that might look the same to us. This was especially true when it came to a favorite toy, whether it was a blanket, a doll, or an old rattle. Around this time, if your baby loses a favorite toy, he'll drive you crazy until you find it. Nothing else will do. He knows it inside and out; you can't fool him.

During those times that your baby is really testing your patience, try to look for something positive in his behavior; you may, as we did, stumble across a new development.

Let's see if your baby has this new, highly developed ability to discriminate with his hands. While he's playing with his favorite toy, take it from him and immediately replace it with a similar toy. Can he tell the difference? Does your baby stare at the substitute? Does he paw all over it? Does he pass it in front of his eyes? Or does he simply go back to his old rough behaviors of grabbing, twisting, and shaking the toy?

As you can see, your baby is trying to accommodate or make his behavior conform to external reality. All thinking involves some conformity, or *accommodation.* as well as *assimilation*—the creative function by which we reinterpret and change reality to fit our own ideas. More about the balance between *accommodation* and *assimilation* will be spelled out in Activity 69.

DIARY

_____

_____

_____

_____

_____

_____

GUIDE

Your baby may know his favorite toy so well that he'll immediately reject the substitute, and you won't get the chance to see him carefully examine it. If this is the case, then give him a new toy which he's never seen before. This should draw out all his careful, sensitive rubbing and poking.

65. THE PLAYPEN

We finally got to the point where we couldn't let Erin out of our sight even for a second. With her newfound mobility—part walking, crawling, stumbling, and tripping—she was a threat to anything in her wake as well as to herself. Unless she could be under constant surveillance, the safest place for Erin was the playpen. She didn't mind it at all just as long as we stayed within sight.

However, don't get trapped into thinking that the playpen is a suitable baby sitter. Your baby still needs you; don't stick your baby in a playpen and forget about her. She'll be the first to sense that you're drifting away, and she will probably try to regain your attention by dropping toys out of her playpen. Stay near by so you can hand back some of these toys and, more importantly, so you can observe the development of a new intellectual skill.

For the first time, the baby sees toys as being unique or as having their own nature, independent of what she does to them. Earlier, your baby felt that a ball rolled and a block dragged because of the way in which they were handled. That's all changed. Now she realizes that no matter how a block is handled, it will never roll like a ball. The toy's nature determines what it can and cannot do, not the way you handle it.

Your baby is beginning to realize that in order to get the most out of a toy, her actions have to fit the toy's nature exactly. So your baby spends a lot of time adjusting her actions while pushing, dropping, sliding, launching, and throwing different toys. Dropping the toys has two functions. It keeps you close, thus making her feel emotionally secure; and intellectually, it provides the baby with a basic understanding of how to control the flight of different objects through space.

Watch what happens when you give your baby a number of different toys. Does she merely shove some to the floor? Does she drop others from delicately opened hands? Maybe she just rolls a few off her finger tips? Does she hurl any to the floor like spears? Does she work on getting the right grip before dropping or launching a toy?

As she accommodates to the toys, your baby is also gaining a basic understanding of how objects fall. This understanding will be helpful when the baby starts developing her ideas about gravity in Activities 70, 71, 72, and 73.

DIARY

GUIDE

If your baby isn't dropping her toys in different ways, then you do it: She may imitate you.

66. CLINGING AND CRYING

Although Christopher hadn't seen his grandmother for nearly a month, as soon as she stepped into the living room, he happily squealed "Gan-Gan!" However, as I moved to greet her, Christopher bellowed a frantic cry and anchored himself to my leg. He wouldn't let me go. Apparently, he felt that I was leaving him in order to be with his grandmother.

Around this time, babies begin to realize that you, as well as toys, are independent of their actions. Now I can come and go as I wish. Before, it was our baby's belief that yelling, banging his head, or kicking would bring me running. But now, operating on a higher level of reasoning, he's forced to see that I don't necessarily have to come. In fact, I may be too far away to hear him. Christopher can't cope with this. That's why the slightest sign that I'm leaving triggers off his crying and clinging. For example, just putting on a hat or standing up may be enough to set off this alarm.

While holding your baby, try two things: Put on your coat, and then place her favorite toy a little out of reach. Does she show any interest in the toy? Does she try to reach for it? Does she push your hand towards it? Or does she seem frozen in her tracks and torn between clinging to you and going after the toy?

Earlier, once you were gone, the baby stopped thinking of you. But now, with a more developed idea of *object concept,* she can still think about you after you've left. This might lead to feelings of abandonment. As she matures, these feelings can be appeased, as is shown in Activity 91.

DIARY

_____

_____

_____

_____

_____

_____

_____

_____

GUIDE

Now take off your coat and see how your baby's reactions change. She's relieved. She knows that you're staying, so now she can concentrate on getting her toy.

67. SNEEZES AND COUGHS

I was convinced that Erik had inherited my hay fever. He started coughing, sneezing, and wheezing just about two weeks ago when I began.

However, we soon spotted an interesting connection. His attacks would intensify as I prepared to leave the house and then would die out a few minutes after I had gone. On top of this, our little boy would often break out in huge rolls of laughter in the midst of one of his attacks.

Finally we put it together. Unlike Christopher before him, who clung and cried whenever I left, Erik coped by imitating my sneezing. Now our little boy is capable of imitating most of my behaviors and little quirks. It is as if he has found a way of keeping part of me with him at all times, even when I am gone. Erik is using his intellectual ability to imitate in order to satisfy an emotional need of attachment.

During earlier stages of development he couldn't imitate my nose-wrinkling, eye-blinking, lip-licking, or anything that involved parts of his body he couldn't directly see. Now, however, he can.

Have your baby imitate some gestures you're making involving eyes, nose, mouth, and tongue. Will he copy you sticking out your tongue? Can he copy your waving bye-bye?

All these little actions show how well your baby can imitate. In Activity 95, he'll be able to produce imitations from memory without your being present.

DIARY

_____

_____

_____

_____

_____

_____

_____

_____

_____

GUIDE

Put a mirror in front of your baby as he tries to imitate you. Seeing his own image may cause him to do more and better imitations.

68. THE FIRST WORD

Leave it to Erin: Her first word was a "No!" It was the word she heard most often when being scolded. Such words are easily picked up and imitated because they're generally associated with highly charged situations like spankings or arguments.

Although the rest of her day may be tranquil and filled with good language, your baby always seems to retain that one instant of over-heard profanity and then rocks the household by coming out with, "Hi, blankety-blank da-da!"

This is an excellent reason to bite your tongue while disciplining children, because anything said or done at the time casts a lasting impression. Contrast these emotionally charged episodes with those rather dull and formal occasions set aside for teaching proper vocabulary and you'll see why your little girl might choose the profane over the proper.

To help your baby develop language, inject a little humor and emotion into the process. First write up a list of the sounds she makes, such as "Ga-Ga" or "Ta-Ta"; then try to blend them into words—for example, garden, garter, tap, and tab. Finally, while saying the words, try playing hide and seek, tickling her, changing your voice, making funny noises, and so on. What are her reactions?

You can see that your baby is beginning to develop speech. With Activity 89, you'll be able to see how much advancement she has made in this area.

DIARY

_____

_____

_____

_____

_____

GUIDE

Put strings of sounds together and see how many your baby can copy (e.g. *a, ba, ca, da,.* . .). Or try singing sounds or words such as the abc's. This may really help her imitation.

69. THE FLYING BROOM

Last week, Christopher learned how to walk. This week, he wants to fly. If he's not spreading his arms like wings, he's sitting on the broom and rocketing through the house.

Christopher is coordinating his walking with a new intellectual ability—pretending. This coordination brings a shift in toys. Now Christopher is into big stuff such as slides, jungle gyms, tubes, and tunnels—objects which, like the broom, often become props for his imagination.

This is a good time to get your baby out of the house and into open spaces where he can really open up his legs—and his imagination.

Since the baby is just beginning to pretend, it's awfully easy to miss out on his development if you fail to look at the world from his point of view.

As this stage rolls to an end, it finds your baby racing ahead into new forms of thinking. For instance, if your're playing a piano, now he can pretend to do the same by drumming on a table. Pretending shows two things: First, that he can imitate your actions, and second, that he can use symbols. His mind, through images, can change the table into a piano and use it as such.

Let's see if your baby can pretend. As he's sitting on your lap, slowly dial the phone. Does he simply stare at you? Does he reach for the phone? Does he imitate your dialing by waving his hands in small circles? Or does he imitate your handling of the receiver?

Being able to pretend means that your baby is *assimilating,* or using his ability to transform reality to make it fit with his own ideas about the world. *Assimilation* and *accommodation* are both needed for intellectual development. The relationship between the two will be discussed in Activity 83.

DIARY

_____

_____

_____

_____

_____

GUIDE

The phoning activity may be too hard because your baby doesn't have a prop, like the table in the piano example, to use in his pretending. So you might have to supply a block or a paper tube that he could pretend to use as a phone. Notice if he scratches the block. This scratching may be his way of dialing.

stage

five

EXPERIMENTING

Twelve to Twenty Months

To say that your baby is a year old and is beginning to walk or talk is accurate enough, but it's only half the picture. To say that this age witnesses a dramatic change in the child–parent relationship is also true, but it is still not the whole story. But what's truly revealing is to watch those thoughts that have been bottled up in your baby's mind for the last twelve months suddenly come alive and explode in the form of throwing food, ransacking closets, playing with toilets, and the like. Such behaviors are usually dismissed as antics intended to test your breaking point. Yet in fact, they are serious undertakings, if not experiments, aimed at testing physical laws such as gravity, trajectory, inertia, momentum, and a long list of others.

Admittedly, this isn't the way you and I would handle such concepts. But that's just the point; we're not babies. Babies live in one world, and we in another. Unless we bend and try to see their viewpoint, there's bound to be a lot of misunderstanding and hard feelings on both sides.

Take the baby who is scolded for breaking an antique. Most damage to property results not from maliciousness but from sheer zeal to show off a new ability. Your baby simply is not smart enough to think that breaking a prized possession is a way to get even with you; that comes a little later in life. Or how about the young child who's punished for climbing out of her crib? This maneuver should be appreciated for what it really is: a high level accomplishment reflecting such things as agility and the ability to maintain body balance, as well as the intellectual capacity to understand that the crib's railing, like a ladder, is a means to an end.

Still, you can't put up with such acrobatics all night. But give your baby some leeway. Don't immediately choke off anything that appears mischievous. Often, if such play is treated as devious, your baby will soon start acting as she is treated. As a result, much of your baby's play can become less an act of constructive intelligence and more a game to see just how far you can be pushed.

So, permit your baby some time to practice and enjoy her new developments. Such an approach has to be anchored in respect, since the purpose of her actions won't always be clear. Try not to be suspicious of her motives; allow your baby the benefit of the doubt.

Unless respect is present, normal development could be viewed as rebellion rather than as independence. If there's anything this stage abounds with, it's independence and self-assertion. Your baby is walking and talking more, giving up some of his naps, helping himself at meals, and setting his own pace in toilet training. Added to this is a new understanding of physical laws which opens to the baby fresh ways for experimenting with and exploring his world. Emotionally, he's also experimenting by testing and probing you. There's a lot of give and take. He can have fun with you, but you can also be overrun by being drawn into one of his games.

A good point to remember during this stage is that the very things your baby needs in order to thrive and develop are the very things that can drive you mad.

70. THE TOY BOX

Tired of seeing Christopher's room looking like a battlefield strewn with broken cars and fallen dolls, to say nothing of those hundreds of little blocks and wheels buried in the rug like booby traps awaiting my tender bare feet, I decided it was time for a toy box. After spending an entire afternoon sifting through the debris and packing it away, I was stunned as Christopher came home from his grandmother's, marched to his room, stared at the box, and began to empty it. Not content simply to pull out toys one at a time, he whipped them out as if he were going for a world's record.

At this age, all our kids have seemed as if they were heading for the record books as being the most contrary of creatures. But in this case, at least there was a plausible explanation for Christopher's behavior. He was beginning to experiment with the concept of gravity by constantly letting things go. Interested neither in watching the toys fall nor in making sure they landed in certain places, Christopher's sole preoccupation, as of now, was simply to throw or to release toys into the air.

To help your baby develop this concept and to save yourself a lot of aggravation, pack a couple of small cartons with toys. Your baby can empty these, while the majority of his playthings can be kept in a big chest somewhere out of sight.

Let's take a look at how your baby's concept of gravity is developing. Drop a little ball. Will he do the same? Does he watch it fall? Or does he merely examine his hand? When the toy hits the floor, what does he do? If you again hand him the ball, does he drop it any differently?

This activity shows the child working out the preliminary experiments he needs in order to understand gravity. Such experimenting is the chief intellectual behavior in Stage 5.

DIARY

_____

_____

_____

_____

_____

GUIDE

Are there some toys which your baby will drop and some he won't? New toys? Old ones? Those that are hard? Soft? Round? Or flat?

71. THROWING FOOD

Most people find it hard to believe that throwing food reflects an intellectual achievement. If anything, it looks like a blatant act of defiance. In reality, both interpretations may be correct. The clue lies in your baby's face. If she looks up and smirks, then you know you're being had. On the other hand, a serious and intense expression indicates that the throwing is a means of understanding a new concept—*trajectory*—the flight of an object in space.

Acts of defiance have to be curbed. Although a stern "No!" or the removal of her food should stop such throwing, a compromise might be more fitting. Tie a little car to her chair with some string. In this way she can eat her food and still have something at hand that can be thrown and easily retrieved. As means are taken to make meals more manageable, we should also be encouraging the baby's development of trajectory by playing with her in certain ways.

While she is sitting in her chair or standing up, drop a block in front of your baby; then hand it to her. Does she let it go? Rather than just inspecting her hands, does she follow the path of the falling object? Does she try to see where it lands? If the block lands under a chair, does she stretch and try to look for it? If so, this shows your baby has grasped the idea of trajectory: Now she follows the block from its beginning to its final landing place.

What this throwing indicates is that your baby is testing out her ideas about trajectory. Once this concept is fully grasped, she'll be able to influence the flight of objects through space.

DIARY

_____

_____

_____

_____

_____

_____

GUIDE

Give your baby the chance to drop the block with either hand. Does she favor either hand? Does she throw the block with a different force each time? Does your baby vary her style of throwing, like a baseball pitcher?

72. NAPKINS

Erin was becoming quite grown up at the table: She drank from a cup, used a spoon, and insisted on having a paper napkin. Her table manners were flawless until one morning she accidentally dropped the napkin and became captivated by its fluttering to the floor. Our baby had discovered air resistance. Up to this point, all the items she had been dropping were heavy cars and blocks that crashed to the floor like lead weights. Now, in these feather thin slices of paper, Erin had found an object that would glide and swoop before gently brushing the floor in a three point landing.

Drop a sheet of writing paper to the floor. Hand the paper to your baby. Will she drop it? Does she merely release it, or does she throw it with force? Does she try to guide it to a certain landing place? Does your baby follow the path of the paper as it flutters downward?

Through this type of play, your baby is beginning to understand that there are invisible forces beyond her control, such as air resistance, which also affect the course of an object. At around three years old, children begin to believe that objects are made to move through space not only due to air pressure and gravity, but also because of personal reasons. Thus, it's common to hear a child say that "clouds move to get away from the hot sun," or that "leaves fall to make blankets for squirrels." This is normal thinking for the preschooler; it's called *animism*. Such thinking involves a mixture of *logical* and *magical* *reasoning*.

DIARY

GUIDE

Give your baby some differently weighted objects to drop. Does she adjust her throwing to the different types of objects?

73. BEANED WITH A BOTTLE

When finished with his bottle, Erik had the habit of throwing it with great gusto. This was a harmless activity unless you were within six inches of him; then you could count on getting beaned. We could never get Erik simply to drop his bottle. Apparently anything big or heavy like a bottle, instead of being dropped, had to be launched into space.

As do most babies during this stage, Erik is confusing inertia with gravity. He believes that a big item, if not catapulted, pushed, or launched, will merely remain suspended in mid-air. He also believes that if an object in flight is grabbed abruptly and held tightly, it can be brought to rest in space.

For example, hold a block against the wall. Next have your baby do it. Will he press or stick it on the wall for a few seconds? Then does he let go of the toy? Is he surprised to see the block fall? Does it appear that he believed the block would remain affixed to the wall? If so, this demonstrates more confusion about inertia.

Here's another example. Roll a ball, and then give it to your baby. Does he merely put it down and think the ball will roll by itself? If so, he doesn't understand that in this case a push is needed to overcome inertia.

As the baby goes through this activity, remember that he's just beginning to understand that gravity has the same effect upon all objects regardless of whether they're big or small, heavy or light. It's a difficult concept to master because gravity is an abstraction and the child is still concrete in his thinking. He can deal only with tangibles. It won't be until he's ten or eleven that your child really can come to grips with an abstract principle such as gravity.

DIARY

_____

_____

_____

_____

_____

_____

_____

GUIDE

If the block and ball activities seem easy for your baby, try the following: Float a ball in a pan of water, then sink it by pressing down on the ball. Can your baby do this? Does he seem to understand that the ball will stay submerged only if it's pressed down?

74. THE COWBOY

Christopher loved T.V. so much that he would often sit in front of a blank screen when the set was off. His favorite shows were cowboy programs, and he would go through all their antics except twirling a lasso. This was out of his range. Rather than rotating his arms he merely shook and jerked them as if snapping a whip.

Fortunately, he found an old pendant necklace and stumbled across the principle of *centrifugal force.* When he shook this heavily weighted necklace, it was virtually impossible not to start it swirling like a lasso.

Attach a little car to a piece of string, and then tie the string into a loop. Swing it like a lasso, and then let your baby try it. Will he do it? Next, rotate it around your wrist. Can your baby do this? After seeing you do it, can he hold the string over his head and whirl it around?

During this activity, your baby is trying to use the string as a specific means to accomplish a specific end. Earlier, he was content with merely being able to move an object by tugging on a string. But during this stage, satisfaction will come only when the child accomplishes his specific end, which in this case is twirling the string. Since his play is much more purposeful now, the child will take a lot of time and go through many trials until he gets what he wants. Later, as shown in Activity 92, such complex play will be mastered in far less time mainly because the child will be using *symbolic reasoning.*

DIARY

_____

_____

_____

_____

_____

_____

_____

_____

GUIDE

To see if your baby really understands the idea of centrifugal force, try the following: Repeat the above activity, but this time hand him the car instead of the string. Does he realize he must hold the string rather than the car? Does he release the car and grab the string?

75. PLAYING CARS

Erik is just starting to take a genuine interest in cars. Earlier, he really didn't even know how to play with such toys. Rather than smoothly pushing, he would press down on the car, almost grinding it into the floor.

Erik's problem was that he didn't understand the concept of *momentum,* thus causing us the problem of floors scratched and marred with rubber skid marks. He didn't understand that he had to push the car and then let go in order to get it to move on its own.

To solve our problem and to help Erik learn that momentum, we tried the following:

Get a hard cover book and some little cars and trucks. Rest a car on the book. Does your baby press down and grind the toy? Now open the cover a bit so the toy is resting on top of a slight incline. Just a slight touch on the car by your baby should cause it to roll forward. Does this happen? What is his reaction? Play with this incline a few more times. Then close the cover. Does your baby still just give the car a little tap? If he starts using the incline, this means he's truly grasped the idea of momentum.

While playing with the car and book, the baby learns about relationships: He learns that a steep incline causes the car to move speedily downward. This is *relational thinking,* or the ability to understand that some objects are linked together in a cause and effect chain. Such thinking is cultivated and refined over the next several months until very complex relational problems can be easily handled. See Activity 93.

DIARY

_____

_____

_____

_____

_____

GUIDE

If your baby seems to have no trouble rolling wheeled toys down an incline, try using something flat such as a block instead of the cars. Does he know how to get momentum going with such an object? Does he tilt the book cover higher now than when he played with the car? Or does your baby return to pressing and crushing the toys?

76. BUILDING TOWERS

This is the time to remove from your closets and cabinets any harmful products such as moth balls, soaps, detergents, scouring pads, and paints as well as glass and other breakable containers. The reason for this is that if your baby is like Erin she will be in and out of every closet and cabinet in the house, scavenging books, pots, pans, boxes, and cans to use for building towers.

Erin could lose herself for many minutes at a time building and knocking down these towers. Each time a new piece or floor was added, she would immediately lean sideways to get a perspective, and she would then lurch back if she sensed the tower was about to top-ple. At times she would sabotage her creations either by knocking out a piece or by just plain shoving over the entire structure. During such episodes, Erin was experimenting with the tower's structural proper-ties in much the same way engineers design and test models.

If you can stand the clutter, let your baby freely construct these towers. Although she can easily keep herself busy with such projects, it would be a good idea from time to time for you to get involved with her in such building. In addition to giving you an understanding of the workings of your baby's mind, such play will also provide you with insight into how your baby handles frustrations and failures, such as when the tower unexpectedly comes crashing down.

Supply your baby with a number of different building materials: blocks of different sizes and shapes, books, balls, cars, combs, paper tubes, and the like. Does your baby seem to have a plan in mind? Does she constantly use the same materials for the foundation? Does she realize that a book can't be laid on top of a ball? Does she build the same basic structure over and over again? When the tower topples, is it the result of an experiment or is it clumsiness?

In building the towers, your baby is manipulating variables. Every time she adds a new block to change the tower, she's introducing another variable. As you can see from this and other activities, much learning can be sparked from very little. Your baby doesn't need elaborate toys. All she needs is what's already around the home: a few odds and ends such as string and blocks, and, most important, some of your time.

DIARY

_____

_____

_____

_____

_____

_____

_____

_____

GUIDE

If your baby really is experimenting with different structures, then see how high she can make a tower. Get a bunch of blocks and start putting up your own tower next to your baby's. Can she copy the height of your tower? How high can she go? If you build a pyramid, can she imitate this?

77. PLAYING BALL

Babies have minds of their own; and they can easily sidetrack you into believing that they want one thing when they really want something else. Take Christopher. He looked like a natural ball player, for he would effortlessly imitate all the moves and subtleties of the pros he watched on T.V. But when I took him out to play, he couldn't do anything. Christopher's idea of playing catch was to drop the ball and hope that it would roll to me.

Obviously he was mimicking the ball players to get my attention. There was no carryover to the game itself. In fact, he immediately lost interest once we started playing. What fascinated him was that the ball could roll down the driveway but could not travel through the grass.

Often we can get so caught up in our own expectations, such as having a child learn to play ball, that we never see the really significant things. For example, Christopher's fascination with the grass may have distracted him from baseball, but it led him to a valuable discovery of *physical resistance.* That is, he learned that some surfaces help while others hinder the path of a moving object.

Whenever you play with your baby, let him take the lead. Be a companion rather than always being a coach, policeman, or teacher. Enjoy your baby. Follow up on what he wants to do, not on what you want him to be.

Here's an activity on *surface resistance* that's right on your baby's level. Gather the following materials: golf, tennis, and ping-pong balls; a terry cloth towel; a small shag rug; and a glossy plastic book cover or placemat. Spread out the towel and try to roll one of the balls across it. Spread the towel on the floor, and have your baby try to drop a ball onto it while he's sitting on your lap or in his chair. What's his reaction when the ball fails to roll or bounce on the towel?

Does he again attempt to drop it, this time using more force? Gradually introduce all the other combinations, using the different balls with the rug and plastic sheet.

With this activity, you can observe your baby experimenting with the concept of resistance. Earlier in this stage, he discovered a rather abstract form of resistance in air pressure. Now your baby can again deal with the concept of resistance, but on a more direct and tangible level.

DIARY

_____

_____

_____

_____

_____

GUIDE

Place the rug and the plastic sheet side by side. Does your baby deliberately try to drop the ball on either one? Does he alternate between the two surfaces?

78. TOILET PLAY

Whenever Erin was quiet, we knew where to look for her: in the bathroom, where she would be splashing in the toilet bowl. There is no mysterious attraction to the toilet. If she could have reached the sink, she would have gone there for her water play. But, as in most homes, the toilet is the most available source of water, so this is where she can experiment with concepts such as *displacement.* Clearly, Erin did not understand that her hand displaced its weight in water. However, such splashing lays the foundation for an eventual understanding of such a concept when the child grows older.

If, for sanitary reasons, toilet play disturbs you, then make a little plastic tub or sink of water available to your baby. In warm weather the garden hose becomes a matchless toy. Whatever you do, never leave your baby alone when she's playing with water, especially if she's playing in a tub of water.

The following activity will give your baby a chance to experiment with displacement. Fill a balloon half-way with water. If you press one end of the balloon, the water will back up into the other end.

Does your baby press one end of the balloon? Does she realize that she is displacing the water in the balloon? Does she alternately tap on each end of the balloon as if it were a tom-tom? This shows that she has some idea about displacement. Another sign of understanding occurs when she grips both ends and causes the middle of the balloon to bubble.

In her water play, your baby is developing some of the basic ideas involved in *conservation.* By squeezing the balloon, she can keep changing its shape and the shape of the liquid in it, yet the balloon and the water still keep their identities. The fact that they remain the same despite these changes in shape is not really understood, conceptually, until around age seven. But this kind of early play paves the way for such an eventual understanding.

DIARY

_____

_____

_____

_____

_____

GUIDE

Playing with a rubber band is another way of experimenting with displacement. Hang different toys onto the band. Does your baby carefully study the rubber band as the toys spring up and down?

79. TUGGING AT YOUR LEG

It was soon after her first birthday party that tugging became Erin's chief means of communicating with us. Almost as if I were on a leash, she would yank at my pants' leg to follow her.

Especially if you're already involved in something, this tugging can be a big annoyance. But take heed; it is also the sign of a big achievement. Your baby has just mastered the concept of tugging at or pulling over to herself blankets and pillows upon which rest toys that would normally be out of reach.

During Stage Four, if she saw a doll on the end of a blanket, your baby would simply wave and beat her arms; but now she'll tug on the blanket until the toy is moved close enough for her to grab it.

Lay a towel on a table so that it drapes partially over one edge. Then put a car or truck on the end of the towel which is farthest away from the table's edge. Does your baby first try to stretch for the car? Then does she bang and wave her arms? Or does she immediately go to the towel and start pulling it? Once the toy moves, does she stop tugging and start stretching for it? Does she snap or jerk the towel as if it were a barrier she was trying to knock down? Does your baby systematically pull and know just when to stop?

Here the towel is being used as a means or instrument for reeling in the toy. In Stage 6 your child gets to the point where she can even improve upon the instruments that she finds. See Activity 92.

DIARY

_____

_____

_____

_____

_____

GUIDE

A real test to see if your baby truly understands the relationship between pulling the towel and getting the toy is the following activity: Hold the car slightly above the towel. Does she notice that the toy is not on the towel? If she pulls and the toy doesn't approach her, does your baby completely stop tugging?

80. PEANUT BUTTER

If Erik had to choose one food to subsist on for the rest of his life, it would, without any doubt, be peanut butter sandwiches. He was crazy over them—with one minor exception: he didn't like the crust. So with every sandwich, after consuming half of it, Erik would wiggle his fingers into its core and try to scoop out the peanut butter. In this way he could avoid eating the crust.

Although far from being ideal table manners, this behavior was interesting because it showed that Erik had not yet grasped an understanding of the spatial concept, "on top of." Our baby did not realize that simply by removing the top slice of bread, the peanut butter would be accessible.

Gather three blocks, two with a natural wood finish and one that's colored green or red. Now pile the blocks, putting the colored one in between the others. Can your baby get out the middle block? How does he do it? Does he knock over all the blocks? Does he try to poke out the middle one? Or does he lift off the top block?

To do this activity, the child must be able to understand three spatial concepts; top, middle, and bottom. In Activity 97, your baby can practice expressing the words to describe these concepts.

DIARY

_____

_____

_____

_____

_____

_____

_____

_____

_____

GUIDE

To make this activity easier, take off the top block. Then, as your baby reaches for the colored one, snap the top one back into place. Does your baby then remove the top block?

81. MOMMY'S LITTLE HELPER

Erik was constantly underfoot, weaving in and out of our legs as we tried to get things done. Every place we went, he tagged along, hoping to be of some help as we cleaned the house. Of all the chores we did, he took most to dusting.

One morning his dust cloth was left right in front of an antique clock that was sitting on a bureau. Erik, trying to move the clock closer, realized that pulling on the dust cloth was not working. So he started pulling and tugging on the bureau scarf, on top of which the clock was resting. Before we could reach Erik, the clock had shattered on the floor.

Our first impulse was to jump all over Erik and scare the dickens out of him. But our baby was already scared, crying, and sorry. He knew he had done wrong and that we were mad, and if Erik could have replaced the clock, he would have.

Breaking a clock is nothing in comparison with breaking a baby's spirit, which can happen when the baby is continuously being punished for some mischief. Try to remember that most of the trouble your baby gets into results from his trying to show you some new skill he's just mastered. He doesn't mean to cause you a problem.

In this case, Erik was showing us that he understood the spatial concepts of top and bottom. During Stage 4, the scarf would have been considered merely an extension of the dust cloth, and the baby would have thought that pulling the cloth would move the clock. Now he realized that the dust cloth was on top of the scarf and that by pulling on the latter, the clock could be brought within reach.

Lay a pair of adult pants on a table with the cuffs near your baby. Then lay a shirt on top of the pants so that it covers them from the knees to the cuffs. Place a little car near the pants' waist. What does your baby do? Does he stretch for the toy? Or does he start reeling in the shirt? What happens when the car doesn't move? Now does your baby lift the shirt and start jerking on the pants' legs? This would indicate that the spatial concept of top and bottom is clear to your baby. He realizes that the shirt is on top of the pants and that the pants are underneath the car.

Here your baby is coordinating a spatial concept with a causal one. He realizes that the toy must be on top of and also making contact with the pants if the latter are to be used as an instrument or a means for moving the toy.

DIARY

_____

_____

_____

_____

_____

_____

_____

GUIDE

To determine how well your baby understands these new spatial concepts, try the following. Hold the toy slightly above the pants. Now will your baby pull at the pants? Or does he realize that the toy must be on top of and not merely over the pants in order for him to be able to get the toy by pulling the pants?

82. THE HIGH CHAIR

From an adult's point of view, smiling, walking, and talking represent rites of passage that usher the baby into our world. However, for a baby—at least for Erin—the most significant rite was the removal of the tray from her high chair. This meant that she was no longer barred from sharing in our meal—a gesture universally understood as a sign of acceptance and friendship.

Her urge to sit at the table, if not to eat, now markedly changed. I can still see Erin wrestling with the high chair, trying to pull it out from the table so she could get into it. First she would tow the chair, stopping just before it was tipped over. Next she would try to scale its sides, failing because her legs could never vault the chair's high railings or arm rests. Finally, out of frustration, Erin would scream for us. That is, she did until the day she learned to twist instead of tow the chair out from the table. Now the seat was free from the table and easy to mount.

In turning out the seat, Erin demonstrated an understanding of an extremely complex concept known as *rotation.*

The idea of *rotation* led to an understanding of other geometric concepts such as *circumference, diameter,* and the like. Examples of experimenting with these new concepts abound. Observe how often your baby turns over her wagon and other wheel toys to spin their wheels; or notice how she rotates her plate so she can reach food on the opposite side. Rotation is frequently associated with spills as your baby learns to turn her cup while it's still in her mouth. You can prevent such messy scenes by giving your baby a drinking cup that's equipped with a lid and a spout.

To get some feeling for how well your baby's concept of rotation is developing, try the following: Color one side of a paper tube with bright-colored crayons. (Do not use paint. It may be toxic and can really harm the baby.) Show your baby the colors, and then hand her the tube with the colored side to the back. What does she do? Does she try to crane her neck around the tube to see its colors? Does she bang and shake the tube? Perhaps she drops the tube and picks it up on its colored side? Or does she rotate it?

The ability to rotate reflects an early understanding of geometry. It implies some notion of circumference. The child is beginning to grasp the fact that she can start at a point and then travel around a surface and end up at her starting point. She is beginning to realize that space has curves; she no longer thinks of it as being only linear. She won't understand these ideas in these terms for some years, but her understanding begins with these kinds of experiences.

DIARY

_____

_____

_____

_____

_____

_____

_____

GUIDE

If your baby has trouble with the tube, maybe this activity will be closer to her level: Tape some shreds of colored paper on the end of a ruler. Then hand her the other end. How does she get to the paper? By dropping the ruler? Or by rotating it down?

83. EYEGLASSES

Around this time, Christopher was growing leery of strangers or visitors he didn't know. That is, unless they happened to wear glasses. If you wore glasses, then Christopher would sidle up to you and signal to be picked up. Once he was in your lap, his hands would gradually snake up to your glasses and try to rip them off your face. At this point, we would rescue the poor person and return his glasses to him. Occasionally, Christopher was faster than we were and managed to get the glasses on himself by clamping his hands over his ears to keep the frames in place.

Finally we found a pair of old frames. But no longer did Christopher clamp the glasses to his head. Now it looked as if he was putting on airs. He would point his nose upward and carry his head with just the right tilt to assure balancing the glasses without any hands. Christopher was demonstrating to us that he understood the concept of a *fulcrum*, that is, an object's point of balance.

Put a plastic donut on one end of a ruler and hand the other end to your baby. Can he hold the ruler at the right angle so the donut is balanced on the other end? Does he dip the ruler, causing the donut to fall off? Or does your baby lift it too high, allowing the donut to slide down the ruler?

In this activity, your baby is trying to find the fulcrum or balancing point. An understanding of balance is important for the young child in order for him to cope with his physical surroundings. However, there's another type of balance called *equilibration*, an understanding of which is the key to intellectual development. *Equilibration* means that the child realizes that there must be a balance between what he wants to think and the way things actually are. Fantasy and imaginary play are examples of how the child twists the world to fit his own thinking, while imitation is a case of pure conformity in which the child tries to fit his thinking to match reality.

As mentioned in Stage 4, imaginary play stems from *assimilation* and imitating from *accommodation*. The particular balance struck between these two processes varies with the kind of problem being solved. Some situations, such as Activity 93, demand more imagination while others, such as Activity 95, call for more conformity.

DIARY

_____

_____

_____

_____

_____

_____

_____

_____

GUIDE

If your baby can't accomplish the above activity, then supply him with a book or paper plate upon which a ball or block is resting. Can he hold the book so the ball is balanced and remains on the book? To keep the balance, does he make adjustments by tilting the book from side to side?

84. THE CEREAL BOX

Our kids were hooked on ads very early in life. Christopher, being the oldest, knew every cereal brand that had some prize or toy submerged within its box. Erin would just look on as Christopher would shuffle tiny cars, dinosaurs, or other such trinkets from these boxes. Finally she caught on, and as soon as any cereal box hit the table, screams of fury would flow out as she demanded to have her chance to search for a prize. Then, like someone sinking her arms into a basin to sprinkle water on her face, Erin would reach into the box. But, she would end up sprinkling the kitchen floor with hundreds of toasted, puffy, sticky nuggets. Or sometimes she would raise both arms over her head, her hands still stuck in the box, while these sticky nuggets rained down on her.

Even when the toy was snared, she had no idea of how to get it out of the box. Her hand cupped around the toy was simply too fat to pull out of the box. If she opened her fist, then the toy would sink further down into the cereal. The solution lay either in spilling out the contents or in guiding the toy up the side of the box with a finger.

On Erin's level, here was a problem as complex as any an engineer would tackle. It required her to have an understanding of some principles of physics, mechanics, and properties of space, not to mention the ability to represent all this symbolically, since she could see neither her hand nor the prize, both of which were buried in the box.

See how well your baby can handle such a problem. Put a tiny car or a figure inside a large 10″ by 12″ business envelope. Does your baby stick her hand in the envelope, groping for the toy? Can she pull out the car? Does she wedge the car up the side of the envelope? Does she ever consider spilling out the toy?

Here your baby is trying to coordinate her hand with a *symbolic image*, that is, a picture in her mind of the object and her hand's action on it. As she plunges her hand deeply into the envelope, your baby must form a mental image representing what her hand is doing and how this relates to getting out the toy. There may be many trials, but eventually she's able to solve this problem.

This kind of problem-solving during Stage 6 may become difficult, because that period of development is a transition in which your baby is moving from infancy to young childhood. During such a chaotic time, which is fraught with change and uncertainty, the child's self-concept often takes a nose dive, as is seen in Activity 100.

DIARY

_____

_____

_____

_____

_____

GUIDE

If this activity is too much of a challenge, try dropping a clothespin into a plastic bottle. Since the bottle is transparent, this might help your baby to visualize the problem.

85. THE TELEPHONE

For Christopher, the ring of the telephone signaled the start of a race. Abandoning everything, he would zoom to the phone as it clanged on its cradle. We bought Christopher a toy phone and even invited him to speak on our phone, but neither ever intrigued him as much as stretching out the coiled wire as we talked on the phone. Soon we noticed that in addition to telephone cords, Christopher was also unraveling the coiled wires of the vacuum cleaner, spools of thread, and even rolled up newspapers.

In his own way, Christopher was experimenting with one of the axioms of science, *conservation:* A substance remains the same even if its shape is changed. In this case the cord is still a cord whether it is uncoiled or rolled up.

During the years between eight and twelve, your child will discover in depth how conservation applies to numbers, space, time, liquids, solids, and so forth. Once a child fully understands conservation, he will be on the brink of thinking symbolically—as adults do. Although such thinking doesn't surface until early adolescence, its roots can be traced back to various infant behaviors, such as playing with the phone cord.

If your baby understands conservation to some extent and realizes that a string is still a string even if it is coiled up, then he'll have no trouble hauling in a toy that's attached to a string. To get an idea of how well your baby grasps this early form of conservation, try the following: Tie a doll to one end of a string, and then twist the string like a snake across a table. Give your baby the empty end of the string. Does he pull the string? Does he keep his eye on the toy's movements? If the toy doesn't budge after his first pull, what does he do? Does he go back to his "magical" jerks and shakes? Or does your baby keep pulling, showing that he understands conservation?

The idea behind this activity is to see if your baby understands that an object is still fundamentally the same even if its shape is changed.

DIARY

_____

_____

_____

_____

_____

GUIDE

If the above play was too difficult, try the following: Attach a toy to a three foot long string. Then spread the string out across the table while keeping it slack. Does your baby seem to understand that this long loose string is the same as one that is short and taut? Does he pull the string?

86. EATING IN A RESTAURANT

Children often have a hard lot because they're in a world run mainly on adult terms. However, such a world can be just as punishing to parents. Take eating in a restaurant. As your party enters, a waitress usually deals each member a knife, fork, spoon, napkin, and menu, along with a tumbler of water. These are the niceties adults have come to expect. Unfortunately, when you are the only two adults in a party of preschoolers, these niceties become nightmares. Inevitably, the water is spilled, a brother is stabbed with a fork, or someone boasts of having two napkins—all of which leads to an all-out civil war!

In most instances, we have gotten to the waitress before it was too late. However, one time we missed getting to her; but it was to our advantage. On this night, Erin did an extraordinary thing. She casually grabbed a fork and extended it across the table, spearing a piece of bread. After we disarmed her, it suddenly occurred to us that she had just wielded the fork like an instrument as a means to an end.

By using the fork in this manner, Erin indicated that she was thinking symbolically. Since the fork was not physically connected to the bread, she had to make the connection in her mind.

See if your baby can symbolically think out a connection between a means and an end. Place a little block out of reach. Then lay by the side of her hand an unsharpened pencil or some other stick-like object that could be used as an instrument. Does your baby use the pencil as a means to reach the block? Or does she just stretch for the toy? Put the pencil in front of her hands. Now does she grab it? What happens if you touch the block with the pencil? Does this give her the idea? What if you touch her hand with the pencil?

Such symbolic thinking, or the ability to bring together in one's mind things that don't actually exist, will become more common in the next stages, as is shown in Activities 96 and 98.

DIARY

_____

_____

_____

_____

_____

_____

_____

_____

_____

GUIDE

If your baby doesn't use the instrument, then place a ruler in her hand. This instrument is so long that, simply by accident, your baby will probably hit the toy and get the idea of using the ruler as a means of reaching the toy.

87. THE BANANA

A couple of weeks after Erin discovered the fork as a means, she dazzled us with the following maneuver. While eating, she tried to use her baby spoon to drag over some crackers. However, the spoon was so short that our baby dropped it and then grabbed a long banana and used it to guide over the crackers.

At this point, Erin was capable not only of thinking symbolically about means but also of making symbolic comparisons between different means, that is, between the spoon and the banana.

Erin knew that this was quite an accomplishment; and she took every opportunity to show off her new ability by playing games such as sticking the banana in Erik's ear. Remember, this is a stage when your baby is so excited over her developments that she'll do anything to get someone to watch her, even if it means teasing and taunting her brother, who already has an acute case of sibling rivalry.

Erin and Erik would fight like cats and dogs. One way to ease this friction was to spend an entire morning alone with just one child. This meant that I would be exclusively his or hers. It was great for the baby's ego, to say nothing of how much closer it brought the two of us.

This rivalry was by no means one-sided. Erin would contest with her big brother for anything: toys, food, or attention. It was amazing that Erin's emergence into this rivalry came just at a point when she could make some high-level comparisons. Now she knew exactly when she was getting the short end of things.

Let's see how well-developed your baby's capacity is to make symbolic comparisons. Place one of your baby's favorite toys out of reach. Put a twelve inch ruler and a toothbrush next to her. Does she merely reach for the toy? Or does she go for one of the instruments? Do you have to point out the instruments to her? Which one does she choose first?

The purpose of this activity is to see if your baby can make comparisons. During "Winding Up," your baby will start to make comparisons that deal with such abstract concepts as time. See Activity 99.

DIARY

_____

_____

_____

_____

_____

GUIDE

Can your baby immediately make the correct choice of instruments among three that are close in size? Place a toy out of reach again, but this time place a comb and an unsharpened pencil with the toothbrush.

88. A BIRTHDAY PRESENT

What do you think of giving pots and pans for a birthday present? Practical maybe, but certainly not glamorous or exciting. That is, unless you're a baby celebrating her first birthday. Then, there is nothing more exciting to receive because, at this time, she has discovered the concept of nesting, that is, how to stack small objects into progressively larger ones. Nesting is a primitive version of *seriation,* or the ability to put things in order according to size.

Watch your baby empty your collection of pans and begin to fit the smaller ones into the bigger ones. If it is not pans, then it's bowls, cups, or ash trays. With this early form of seriation, your baby is getting into multiple comparisons such as big, medium, and small. As a result, people and things can be ranked or put on a scale according to size or some other quality. With seriation comes the foundation of mathematical thinking. It's also a development which permits your baby to show different degrees of affection, tolerance, and anger according to whom she is with. No longer are individuals either liked or disliked. Now your baby can like, love, or adore as well as dislike, deplore, or hate.

Give your baby three differently sized paper cups. Does she fit them together by size? Can she fit them immediately? Or are a few trials necessary? Once she has fit them snugly together, how does she take them apart? By shaking? Or by sliding them out one at a time? The latter signals a higher level understanding of this concept, since now she is able to seriate in reverse.

Remember that the purpose of this play is to determine whether the baby can order objects by size. The ability to seriate several objects is not completely developed until the child is four or five years old. At that time, seriation helps her understand the concept of number.

DIARY

_____

_____

_____

_____

_____

GUIDE

Give your baby five cups. Can she fit these together by size? How many cups can your baby fit together correctly?

89. READING

Christopher is fifteen months old and he reads books; sometimes they're upside down, and sometimes they're right side up. But it really doesn't matter much, because what interests Christopher is pointing to pictures, such as one of an elephant, and then touching his own nose while slurring the word "nuzz."

This represents a new development. Before, you could never get Christopher to imitate any actions that required touching his nose, mouth, ears, or forehead. This was because he couldn't see these parts on his own body. Now if you tug your ear, he can imitate this gesture even though the ear is a part of himself that he can't see.

Thumb your nose at your baby. Can he copy you? What if you touch your chin; can he follow this? Pull your ear lobe and see what the baby does. Scratch the back of your head. Does he imitate this action? Being able to accomplish such imitations indicates that your baby's mind is starting to operate on a symbolic level. He can form a picture in his mind as to where these different parts are, even though he can't see them.

Such play with pictures shows that your baby is able to copy a model exactly. During Activity 95, he'll be able to perform the same imitation but without the model being present. At that time he'll be copying a mental image of the model which is stored in his mind.

DIARY

_____

_____

_____

_____

_____

GUIDE

The next step in imitation is now towards more refinement. The baby will copy you to the last detail. Hand him a pencil upside down. As you begin to write, does he immediately turn his pencil around so it's in the same position as yours, with the eraser on top?

90. OFF TO GRANDMOTHER'S

In preparation for a visit to her grandmother's, Erin was madly stuffing her little valise with such oddities as seven winter hats, four scarfs, three shoes, one sock, and a mitten. As the mound of clothes grew, Erin suddenly realized that she had forgotten her favorite pair of pants. So from the hamper she dug her tiny cowboy jeans with a wide western-styled belt, capped with a rhinestone buckle. The pants were flipped onto the mound, but they quickly slid straight to the floor. They were thrown up two or three more times, but always with the same result. Desperately, Erin switched to a new strategy and started beating, hammering, and pounding the legs of the pants into the mound. When they still slid down because of the heavy buckle, she broke down in frustration and despair.

"Why all the fuss?" I wondered. It seemed to me that Erin was blowing this little problem all out of proportion. Then it struck me.

She and I were looking at the same situation from two very different points of view. If she were ten years older, our differing views would be seen as a classic example of the generation gap. Though it doesn't usually show itself to any great extent until children are older, the gulf between parents and children begins during infancy. It widens every time we fail to consider how our baby might be seeing her world.

In this instance, we had sense enough to back off and try to look at the situation from Erin's point of view. Then, things began to click. Only a few days ago, our baby had just discovered the physical law that a body at rest needs a force to overcome its inertia. But she wasn't pushing, pulling, or applying any such force, and still the pants fell. This inconsistency just overloaded her emotional circuits, causing her to break down with frustration.

Here was a clear-cut example of how the baby's intellectual and emotional development and our own crossed.

To acquire a little more insight into your baby's intellectual development, which may help you to prevent some of her emotional breakdowns, try the following: You will need a business envelope plus an eighteen-inch piece of string to attach to a spoon. Now put the spoon and string into the envelope. Can your baby do the same? Does she just jam in the string? Does the heavy spoon dangle down and pull out the string? Does she ever grab the spoon and thrust it into the envelope?

When doing this activity, your baby will have to coordinate an understanding of gravity, balance, and inertia. At this point, such a coordination requires a lot of time, to say nothing of the endless trials and errors. However, with symbolic thinking, the same feat can be accomplished in a split second, as is demonstrated in Activity 92.

DIARY

_____

_____

_____

_____

_____

GUIDE

If your baby finds this difficult, then shorten the string an inch at a time. How short does the string have to be for your baby finally to get it and the spoon into the envelope?

91. GOING OUT

Erin has an interesting way of reacting to baby sitters. If she wakes from a nap and finds us gone, then Erin will make it miserable for the baby sitter. And when we return, she'll snub us, pretending to be deeply hurt. In contrast, if she's up when we leave, Erin has a good time with the sitter and is happy to see us return.

These two emotional reactions can be traced to a more refined development in *object concept*. Earlier, if a ball were hid first under a cup and then under a napkin, Erin would never search in the second place for the ball even though she had observed the hiding. But during this stage, no matter where I hide the ball, she'll find it just as long as she sees me moving it. The same holds true for my going out. If she can see me leave, then she knows I am still around and will eventually show up.

Seeing me is critical. If I leave, or if I hide a ball without her seeing me, then she has no idea where to look for me of for the toy; both have simply vanished. A missing parent is enough to bring out panic, worry, and feelings of desertion in a baby.

To soften the blow of your absence, tell your baby your plans before she naps, or try to go out while she's awake. If you have to leave during her sleep, then either call back or leave a tape with some reassuring message; just the sound of your voice will soothe her.

Here's a game for your baby that's based on *object permanence*. You need a cup, a bowl, a napkin, and some raisins or flakes of cereal. While your baby watches, hide these morsels first under the cup, then under the bowl, and finally under the napkin. Does your baby look under the napkin? Switch things around so the food is finally hidden un-

der the cup and then under the bowl. Does she still search in the last place? Finally, try a fourth hiding place. Can she follow this?

From this play, you can observe that your baby has really made progress in her ability to understand *object concept*. During Activity 98, she will have taken the final step in achieving a complete understanding of this concept.

DIARY

_____

_____

_____

_____

_____

GUIDE

If a ping-pong ball is put under a napkin, its shape shows through. Your baby may be able to find it without having seen it being hidden. First, put the ball under a cup, and then move it, in full view of your baby, to the bowl. Now, while distracting her, slip the ball under the napkin. When she returns, where does your baby start searching? Does she move to the napkin?

WINDING UP

Eighteen to Twenty-four Months

In many ways your little one still looks like a baby. With her puckish face and wispy hair, she could be in diapers. With her rubbery legs and a shaky gait, she could be in a playpen. Yet she is neither in diapers nor in a playpen, but in the training pants and playgrounds of a young child. During the next few months, your baby will wind up her infancy and march head-on into the age of childhood.

Like any transition, this one is punctuated with mix-ups, flare-ups, and inconsistencies. Your baby is growing up, and you, her parents, are reluctant to let go. Her mind is operating at a fast clip, yet her emotions and speech lag far behind. Although you remain a steady playmate, she's beginning to enjoy the company of friends.

Although there's confusion, one thing definite about the eighteen month old is that she can function on a symbolic level. Any further development throughout life is but a refinement and extension of this function. The mind's capacity at this age is truly phenomenal.

I can remember a normal child of a blind couple trying to avoid being detected by her father. She had bells on her shoes (a device used by her parents so they would be able to tell where she was); and she slowly shuffled and stepped backwards, knowing full well that this would silence the bells. Aware that she was about to "con" her father, the little girl clutched her face, fighting back the impish giggles and laughter that would have betrayed her location.

Being able to understand the acoustical principles needed to quiet the bells is, in itself, impressive, but consider how advanced such thinking is when these principles can be applied to manipulating social situations.

Such a quick mind opens some real advantages to the child, such as solving complex problems with little adult assistance. As a result of this independence, the parent's role changes to that of a manager who keeps the child's learning environment stocked with suggestions and activities. Managing from the sidelines, as opposed to being directly involved with the child, offers a perspective to observe the development of his learning styles or his preferred ways of studying, handling, and dealing with various challenges.

Helping the mind to meet these challenges, the child now has a maturing and well-built body. He runs fairly fast, corners poorly, and prefers to stop by pitching forward like a sprinter lunging for the finish line. Speed seems to be an obsession during "Winding Up," whether in thinking, running, or eating. Food is gobbled by whatever means available, by using spoons or cups, or simply by digging in with the fingers. Now, with a fair number of teeth, and with the jaw muscles fully in control, the child can consume most adult food if it is diced and sliced in appropriately small pieces.

Despite burning up all this energy, the child naps less; but he still logs ten to twelve hours a night. However, his sleep is often shattered with wild nightmares and terrible fears. Such dreams and illusions, like imaginative and make-believe play, stem from the child's growing power of symbolic thinking. Fantasies, imaginary friends, monsters, and phobias occasionally surface, but they really don't emerge with full force until next year.

What you have to deal with now are frustrations. When things now easily thought of in the mind don't come off as smoothly in the real world, the child breaks down. He can't cope with ineptitude, whether it is yours or his. Aware for the first time that he has flaws and limits, the child views himself, at times, in a negative light. It is inevitable that some feelings of worthlessness and inferiority creep into his self-concept.

Although he may sometimes be moody and turned inward, don't be put off and get angry if you can't always deal with your child during this stage.

How do you handle such a child? There are glib and easy answers, but they don't fit hard cases. There are generalizations, but human beings are unique. There are books, but you're not going to find ready-made answers in them.

If you've spent time with your child:

> Playing with her,
> Changing with her,
> Trying to understand her world,
> Then you'll still have questions
> But now you'll know where to go
> For answers — they lie in your child.

"Listen" to your child's words *and* deeds, and look for patterns that suggest typical kinds of situations for which her reactions are predictable. She will "tell" you what she needs.

92. MOUNTAINS TO CLIMB

"Mama-Mama" was Christopher's usual S.O.S. But this time it had a different ring. We traced the call to a steep stair case where, halfway up and swaying to and fro, our little boy was perched. Christopher never would have tried such a feat without an adult before; but today, he had done it alone. Instinctively, I reached for him—only to be spurned as our baby pivoted and continued his ascent to the top. Then, as if having scaled Everest, Christopher turned and raised his arms triumphantly.

In the midst of cheering his success, I was suddenly struck with mixed feelings, if not gloom. He was growing up, and I had feelings both of wanting to let go and of wanting to hold on. His self-sufficiency was showing everywhere. At one time he would have been tugging and jabbering at us to help him carry things, find toys, or open doors. But now he was doing these things himself.

The reason for this surge of independence is that the child now can think of solutions in far less time than it takes to badger and pester you into helping him. Such speedy thinking stems from his ability to reason on a symbolic level.

Once more, you can see how the mind and personality are woven together: A highly symbolic mind breeds autonomy and a different kind of relationship with people. In no way has your child outgrown you. His needs are simply different now. Unless parents shift gears, we won't be able to meet these new needs, and our child will really grow away from us.

To get an idea of your child's new development, try the following play activity: Place a plastic cup on a shelf about eighteen inches away. Then, hand your child one end of a yardstick whose other end is weighted down by having some wooden blocks taped to it. The weight of this end will make the stick unmanageable if the baby tries to extend it to knock over the cup. What's his first reaction? Does the child notice the problem on first picking up the stick? Or does it take him a few attempts at wielding the stick to make this realization? How long before he switches it around to hold the heavy end? Does it happen quickly? Or does he spend time actively experimenting with it?

When the baby switches the stick, it shows that he is *assimilating*, or adapting something in the environment to fit his needs. If he holds the stick as it is given to him, he is *accommodating* himself to the situation or conforming to the requirements of the environment. This problem requires more assimilation than accommodation. All problem solving calls for a balance of assimilation and accommodation, but the exact balance depends on the uniqueness of each problem. This balance is known as *equilibration.*

DIARY

_____

_____

_____

_____

_____

_____

_____

GUIDE

If your child can master the above activity easily, then try the following: Weigh down both ends of the yardstick. This should cause two adjustments: The child may (1) choke up or grip the stick midway in order to gain some leverage or he may (2) use both hands in a coordinated fashion. Does your child rely on either of these or on any other means in order to reach the cup?

93. SLAMMING DOORS

All kids have different calling cards to announce their presence. Christopher constantly talked; Erin stripped, leaving a trail of clothes through the house; and Erik slammed doors.

This wasn't always the way Erik signed in. We first noticed it when Erik began to play with pull toys. It seemed that in the past our screen door would invariably slam and pin to the threshold either the trailing toy or its string. Now, Erik would simply fling open the door and bolt into the kitchen with the toy bobbing at his heels, just missing being slammed by the door as it sprang back.

Although crude by adult standards, this action involves coming up with the most effective plan after combining, analyzing, and testing a complex maze of variables: space, time, length of the string, speed across the threshold, force, tension in the door's spring, and so on. Earlier, such a complex analysis would have boggled the mind. The baby would simply cry, call for help, or try to yank the string through the door. However, now, with symbolic thinking, the mind, in a split second, can comb through all these variables and produce a plan that is both thoughtful and pragmatic: in this case, flinging open the door.

Having a complex mind does have its drawbacks, mainly because the emotions are not as well developed. Thus, the child has little tolerance for slip-ups, whether yours or his. If something goes wrong or doesn't happen on time, he unleashes a tantrum. Because your child is almost two years old, you might expect him to try a little harder. In fact, he's trying too hard and is frustrated when things do not happen as smoothly as his mind can make them happen. So, when dealing with your baby, remember that his sudden flare-ups have less to do with meanness than with an intellect that's outgrown the emotions meant to support it.

Here's an activity to gauge your baby's complex thinking. Have your child stand behind a chair that has spindles for its back. Then place a yardstick horizontally against the spindles so that your child can grab it and pull it against the bars. Does your child try to get the stick through the bars? How? Does he merely drop the stick and then move around the chair to pick it up? Does he slide it along his hands and then slip it at the right angle through the bars? Or does he reach around the chair and grab it? The second solution represents some pretty thoughtful and complex thinking. The first and third, although complex, are more pragmatic than the second solution.

In addition to having unique calling cards, children are now also beginning to show preferred learning styles. Here's an opportunity to see if your child has a particular learning style. Is it thoughtful and reflective? Or right to the point and pragmatic?

This play demonstrates that your child can solve a very complex problem without much trial and error. Earlier, such a problem would have been drawn out and punctuated with many failures, because the child would not have been thinking on a symbolic level. Now, with symbolic thinking, he can do this problem easily.

DIARY

_____

_____

_____

_____

_____

GUIDE

This may offer more of a challenge. Place the stick vertically so that while one end rests on the seat of the spindle-back chair, the other end extends over the chair's back. Now, having gripped the stick, how does your child get it through the bars?

94. HALLOWEEN

It was Halloween week and you could see Erin torn between digging into the treats that were lying around or waiting for what her brothers were billing as "the most spookiest, horriblest, and funnest night ever."

Finally, one afternoon, her will power snapped, and she rushed over to get a trash can to stand on in order to reach the candy. With everything in place, Erin went to mount the can, but she ended up stepping into it instead. She had neglected to turn the can upside down. Extricating herself, Erin immediately surveyed the scene and then raised and dangled her leg as if she were about to strut. For a moment she remained frozen in her strut; then slowly, the leg dropped and she proceeded to turn over the can and snatch a few candies.

Although she was close to solving the problem, Erin lacked the key concept, overturning the can. The solution was finally obtained only by strutting or acting out the answer. This form of intelligence was characteristic of the last stage, when ideas were tested, acted out, or actually experimented with.

This only goes to prove what shaky ground she's on. In this sixth stage—with new language, play, and other development—it's easy to build up some high expectations for your child and then be crushed when they're not met. So don't push your baby. She still has a long way to go, whether in talking, toilet training, or thinking.

Here's a challenging activity that your child may solve either by thinking or by acting out her answer. Get a two inch thick book such as a dictionary, encyclopedia, or telephone directory. Open it three quarters of the way towards the back, near the "R" section, and slip in a book mark so that it's barely sticking out when you close the book. How does your baby get it out? Does she peel the pages and then open the book? Does she dig right into the "R" section? Watch her face and gestures to see if she's acting out a solution. Does she arch her eyebrows or open her mouth to reflect raising or opening the book? Do your child's hands go through any motions indicating that they're acting out an answer to this problem?

As your child is doing this activity, remember to look for any signs of motor intelligence, or the acting out of ideas. Often, during this stage, because symbolic thinking is so new, your child will slip back to older forms of expression involving motor intelligence. There are also occasions when she'll regress emotionally. This is a difficult stage for your child as she leaves infancy and begins to prepare for her next period of development, early childhood.

DIARY

_____

_____

_____

_____

_____

_____

_____

_____

GUIDE

Pack about ten books tightly between two book ends. Then pull out one book; the others should slant to fill up the empty slot you have created. Read the book to your child, and then see if she can return it to its proper place. Does she think or act out her solution?

95. ROLE PLAYING

Erik was my understudy, mimicking everything I did; and he would jump at any opportunity to take over my role. When I cut the grass, he would be there with his toy mower. After closing the door to our house, he would demand the keys so that he could duel with the lock. Just the other day, as I turned off the car and went to open the garage, Erik slid behind the wheel—but not before locking all the doors of the car. Need I tell you how I felt?

I wasn't the only one he would copy. Policemen, doctors, and store clerks were other roles he had down to a tee. Such acting out of different jobs, although primitive, was actually laying down an understanding of the various social roles and functions that he would later grasp on a much higher level. It would be interesting to see if your child imitates more male or female roles at this time.

Such actions flow from Erik's new ability to imitate anything he sees: people, toys, animals, and so on. As a matter of fact, he can even imitate things he's seen in the past: This is called *deferred imitation.*

Read to your baby from one of his favorite books. Then return in a half hour and ask him a question that relates to the story. For example, "Show me how Pooh drinks the honey." Does your baby act out the behavior in question? In about four hours get back to your baby with another question from the same story. Has the quality of his imitation stood up over time? Do the same thing on another day, but with a story he doesn't like. Do his feelings about the story affect his deferred imitations?

This activity concerns *deferred imitation,* or your child's ability to recreate someone's behavior which he saw in the past.

It's during this stage that you'll begin to observe your child imitating what he views on T.V. The biggest fault with television is not so much its content as it is that we often use it as a babysitter to absorb our kids. Like using crib toys, the T.V. cuts down the time you could be spending with your child.

DIARY

_____

_____

_____

_____

_____

_____

_____

GUIDE

If your baby is struggling with the above activity, then try the following. Show him some pictures and ask him to imitate what he sees: "Can you act like this dog?" This form of imitation is known as *representational imitation.* Here, the baby can translate some symbols into immediate actions, while with *deferred imitation* he carried the symbols in his head for an extended period of time.

96. NIGHTMARES

Around this time Erin began to talk a lot to herself before and after falling asleep. Then one night, as the talking trailed off, she suddenly shot out a scream that sheared through the house. The scream was nothing to her frantic slapping and kicking. Only by shaking her and yelling, "Erin, Erin, it's only Mommy and Daddy" could her writhing be calmed. Startled at first, she soon went limp and sank into my arms, falling safely and snugly asleep.

Nightmares are akin to another development during this stage, *imaginative play*. Both these developments distort and twist reality. For example, through play, a pencil can be transformed into a plane, a car, a spoon, a brush, or a rocket. Similarly, an experience with the doctor or a trip to the zoo can be twisted into a nightmare. Imaginative play, like nightmares, is an outgrowth of your baby's ability to think on a symbolic level.

To get an idea of how powerful an imagination your child possesses, try the following. Pretend you're talking with a carrot as if it were a phone. Does your child in any way indicate that she understands what you're doing? Does she laugh? Or perhaps she calls out words such as "talk," "Grandma," "phone," and the like. Try giving her something like a stalk of celery that resembles a carrot. What does she do with it? Does she use it as a telephone? Or does she come up with her own imaginative ideas? If you ask her to write with it, what happens?

This imaginative play you're involved with stems from *assimilation*, the child's ability to transform reality so that it fits his thinking. Such distortions of reality become so powerful that frequently the pre-schooler is confused between what's real and what's made up. This confusion is called *realism*. If you've ever witnessed a child's trauma after a nightmare you know how real it seems to her. To calm the child, it's best to search out the "monster" and go through the motions of tossing it out the window. Your insistence that there isn't a monster in the bedroom won't make sense to the child. But at around four, she'll begin to be able to distinguish easily between dreams and reality.

DIARY

_____

_____

_____

_____

_____

_____

GUIDE

Most of your child's imaginative play up to this point has involved props such as carrots and celery. Can your child create imaginative characters or different feelings without any props? Ask her to act angry, sad, happy, hungry, tired, and so on. Can she pretend to act out these different states and emotions?

97. V.D.

Runny noses, cold sores, coughs, colic, diaper rash, and the like are but a few of the common maladies we've learned to cope with during these first two years. Unfortunately, around this time an affliction shows up in some children for which no known cure exists. Of course I'm referring to V.D. or Verbal Diarrhea: that steady stream of words and utterances from dawn to dusk that infects many babies who are just learning to talk. Christopher had it the worst; in fact it still lingers on today.

Often, such a verbal outpouring isn't taken seriously, and yet it's extremely important to intellectual and language development. It shows that the mind is able to produce ideas faster than they can be expressed. Depending on how it's handled, this verbal overflow can either help or hinder your child's future language development.

Occasionally this overflow is ignored or muzzled, leaving the child to practice by himself without an adult to help shape his speech. When attended to, it's usually the cute things we pick out—such as "plune," a concoction of "plum" and "prune" uttered by Christopher whenever he wanted "fluit" [sic].

Perhaps least helpful to the child is perpetuating his verbal torrent with intermittent nods, encouragements, and elaborations: "Good, Christopher!" "What happens now?" "I didn't know that." Usually, these are half-conscious statements issued when you're on the run, try-ing to do a million things at once. What the child learns from this is to talk as fast as he can, hoping that something he says will strike your attention. He's not really listening to what's being said, and neither are you. If anything, this on-the-run discourse may just kindle the child's egocentric speech habits.

Admittedly, you have a lot to do. Still, language is far too important a development to be left to whenever you have some free time. One way to accommodate everyone is to involve the child in many of the things you do. Assign definite jobs to him and give specific instructions, such as: "Bring over the two pencils"; "I need your socks"; "The green towel is under the table"; and "Carry over the pillows."

When you ask for things, label what you want by saying, for example, "I need the big spoon." See how many colors your child can recognize. Ask him to show you "the blue car," "the green block," and so on. You can help your child fit words to the spatial concepts of top, middle, and bottom during eating times: ask him what's in the middle of his sandwich. See if he can point to the bottom of his cup, the top of the jar, and so on.

Simple exchanges such as these stimulate the development of such concepts as numbers, a sense of property and ownership, color, space, and plurality. Most important, they contribute to helping your child give words to his thoughts, so he can label the environment and his own ideas in terms you both can understand.

Next, see if your child can use and express possessiveness. Ask him, "Whose is this?" Can he use the possessive form, answering "Christopher's" or "Mine?" Does he use hers or his properly?

Now try plurals. Ask "Who rides the bus?" Does he name a series of people or does he say, "Kids." When asked "What's in the big toy chest?" Does your child say "Toys?"

As you get a feeling for your child's verbal ability during this activity, remember that not until he's around ten will be be able to express his thinking fully through language.

Although the child may speak as we do, his ability to reason as we do lags behind.

DIARY

_____

_____

_____

_____

_____

GUIDE

If your child can handle the above, see what he can do with numbers. Ask him to bring one, two, then three, and then four objects. What's his limit? If you show him two balls and ask "How many?" what's his reply? You may also want to try sizes and shapes: "Which one is the big car?" "Can you find the square?"

98. HIDE-AND-SEEK

Erin was really becoming outgoing. She loved to play with her older brothers and all their friends. Happy to be included, Erin was never bothered by always being stuck with the worst parts in such play. In hide-and-seek, for example, she was always "it."

This participation in games signaled new social maturity as well as intellectual developments. During the last stage, Erin didn't have the understanding to play the "it" part. She could block her eyes and spout the countdown, but when she looked up and couldn't see anyone, Erin would break down and cry. Not having seen the kids hide, she believed them to have vanished forever.

Now, even though Erin can't see her playmates hide, she's capable of picturing their location in her mind. This ability is known as *invisible displacement*. It's the last step in the development of *object permanence*. Now that she can represent a picture of anything in her mind, your

child will search for any object that's been hidden or lost just as we do.

This new development also makes it a little easier to leave her, for the child can now grasp the idea that you're not vanishing but that you are going somewhere and will return, or, at least that you can be found.

Here's an activity aimed at practicing invisible displacement. You'll need a napkin, a cup, a small pillow, and a small toy car. While your child is looking, put the toy under the cup. Then, while distracting her, move the toy under the pillow. Does she search under the different hiding places until the car is found? Or does she look just under the last place she saw it hiding? The first approach is the more advanced.

Try another activity on invisible displacement. Take a long sock and drop the toy car to its bottom. Even if she can't touch it immediately, will your child keep searching in the sock for the car? If so, this shows that she has an image or representation in her mind of the toy which guides her, despite the fact that she can neither see nor touch the toy.

Being able to find the car demonstrates that the child has finally conquered the idea of *object concept*. Now she realizes that something can exist even though it can't be seen.

For the next three years, your child will be torn between believing what she sees and believing what she thinks. Her perceptions will tell her one thing, while her intellect will be saying something else. That's why it's so difficult to *conserve*, that is, to realize that an object is the same despite the fact that it looks different when its shape has been changed.

DIARY

_____

_____

_____

_____

_____

GUIDE

This is a real test of *invisible displacement* and *object permanence*. Wrap the little car in a handkerchief, and then put this bundle in a box. Next, cover the box with a pillow, and finally drop a big towel over the pillow. Can your child peel away these layers and retrieve the car?

99. BROKEN PROMISES

As Christopher became more reasonable, we found what seemed to be an effective device for getting him to bed: promising him a treat for tomorrow. Our promises were for small things such as reading *Winnie the Pooh,* going to the swings, or rough-housing.

Once morning broke, Christopher inevitably would be posted at our bed like a sentinel, resolved never to give ground until our promise materialized. If we didn't wake up immediately, he would start the incessant chant: "Let's go now!" "When?" "Before Granny comes?" "Later?" "In a minute?" "What's a minute?"

Through it all you couldn't help but be aware that Christopher was trying to grasp the idea of time. To him, tomorrow meant getting up when it's light. As far as our boy was concerned, a unit of time either had to be a brief interval or it had to have something tangible about it, such as a sunrise or daylight. He had no idea that time could encompass a whole day; Such a meaning was too abstract and remote for Christopher. Thus, unless it is delivered within his appointed time, the promise is considered broken and the child can make your day miserable either until he gets his promise or until he is punished. Even worse, a series of such temporal misunderstandings can shake his trust in you.

Now we make promises that can be carried out within Christopher's time frame and our own. For example, books can be read in bed, or promises regarding the use of a special cereal bowl, spoon, or bib can easily be accommodated into our breakfast routine.

Take a look at your child's concept of time. Read him a story such as *Little Red Riding Hood*, and then question him. "Who came to the house before the wolf?" "Who came after the wolf?" "What's going to happen now?" "Who helps the little girl later?"

During meals you can also investigate time by saying some things like: "You can have your dessert after the carrots." Does he gobble up the carrots? Or at least does he recognize, even reluctantly, that they have to be dealt with?

While you are dressing him, you can ask the child: "What goes on before your pants?" "What goes on after your socks?"

Through these activities, you can get some idea of your child's concept of time. One point to keep in mind is that throughout the preschool years, time is psychological. That is, if the child is having fun, time seems to fly; however, if he doesn't like something, time drags. It's difficult to convince him to come home from a friend's house, because your child will really believe he's been there only a few minutes. Understanding time in the physical sense, as we do, doesn't really come about until age eight or nine. That, then, would seem to be the best age to start teaching time.

DIARY

GUIDE

See if your child can understand the idea of different speeds which are related to time. While pushing some toys, ask him to do it faster. Does he respond? Now request a slower pace. What happens? If you shake something very vigorously, what does he do or say? Frequently, young children confuse "more" with "faster" and "no" with "slow." Is this the case with your child?

100. THE BUBBLE GUM MACHINE

Because of the fascinating effects it produces, Erin was completely captivated by gum machines. But it was being able to operate the machine, even more than the gum, that really intrigued her.

One thing led to another, and soon she was hollering to put the money in the slot. It was pathetic, because she just couldn't do it. No matter how she tried, Erin didn't have the delicate coordination to drop in the coin.

To say the least, she was shocked: Her hands had always come through, but now they had failed. With her lightning-fast intellect, capable of analyzing all possible variables, what else could she conclude other than that since her hands were flawed, by extension, so was she?

Erin judges her self worth in terms of how effectively she can deal with the outside world. It takes a pretty sophisticated intellect to make this judgment and an equally powerful personality to handle it. Unfortunately, the emotions are not up to par with the intellect; thus there are frequent mood swings, ups and downs, and feelings of negative and inferior worth during this stage.

Without doubt, it's a confusing time for all. Some days she'll welcome help; while on other days, she reacts to it as if it were an infringement upon her freedom and independence. The slightest reprimand will bring gushes of tears.

It's a time when you should control your anger, for she's angry enough at herself. It's a time when your role begins to change.

Rather than always playing directly with your child, now you should back off a bit and spend more time making sure things are around or are set up so that she can play on her own.

The following is a good self-learning activity for helping a child develop her skills of fine motor manipulation and coordination. Get a large 10″ x 12″ business envelope, a plastic donut, and a little wooden cube. First put these objects into the envelope, and then remove them. Then, hand them to your child. Does she peel back the flap with one hand and try to shove in the object? Does the hand holding the flap actually block access into the envelope? Does she realize this? Does she make any attempt to hold the envelope upside down and toss the object up into the envelope? Does she try laying the envelope on the floor in order to drive the donut into it?

This activity touches upon two points: the child's ability to perform a task, and how that performance affects her self-concept. If, during the past two years, the child's play has been relatively well matched to her development, then she'll realize her limits and powers. Thus she will neither shrink from a challenge nor bite off more than she can chew. She will know herself in much the same way as you have gotten to know her through *Help Your Baby Learn.*

DIARY

_____

_____

_____

_____

_____

GUIDE

If your child can easily accomplish the above, have her try to put poker chips or playing cards into a regular size envelope. This requires a deft touch in contrast to the above activity.

CONCLUSION

As we reach the end of *Help Your Baby Learn,* you may wonder where to go next. If you've gone through the activities with your baby, you should have learned enough about how he thinks and feels and about what's important to him that you'll be able to start right up, with activities of your own invention, from where we've left off. If you've simply read about the activities, I hope you'll now try them out with some babies. You'll learn a lot more that way, since this book is just a guide: The real teachers are the babies themselves.

From your experience in doing the activities, you have learned (or will learn) many things. One of the most important things I hope you will take away from the experience is that you should not try to rush children into our adult world. They have a world of their own and ways of considering things which are often upside down in comparison with ours. The book's cover which shows a baby looking at the world upside down through his legs is intended to remind you of this.

From the child's world-view, actions such as drooling, thumb-sucking, and patty-cake are important signs of development. unfortunately, most of us are stuck with an adult world-view which tends to consider important only those things, such as walking and talking, which resemble adult behaviors. Only when the baby is accepted on her own terms, and not on ours, will her developments be appreciated.

The key to gaining this appreciation is time. Becoming a good parent isn't easy. Even if all the significant aspects of infant development were pointed out to you, it would still require a lot of work before you could discover those special cues and unique signals used by your baby to show off his achievements.

The assertion that the quality of time you spend with your child is more important than the quantity is not entirely accurate. Whatever you do—dancing, art, sports, cooking, and so on—demands hours of practice before you can ever provide a quality performance. Being a parent is no different. A certain quantity of time is necessary as a foundation for the development of quality in parenthood.

If *Help Your Baby Learn* gets you to spend more time with your baby, it will have done its job. The rest is up to you.

Best of luck from Christopher, Erik, and Erin, who made this book possible; from my wife Mary who gathered most of the observations; and from me, who tried to write it all down.

STEPHEN LEHANE
Department of Early Childhood Education
Kent State University
Kent, Ohio

BACKGROUND
MATERIAL

Here are a number of readings that should give you a feel for some research and its application to child development and parent behavior.

RESEARCH

Obviously these studies don't cover the entire field of child rearing. They're meant only to give you a general idea of what some researchers have been doing in the field.

Ainsworth, M.D.S. Object relations, dependency, and attachment: A theoretical review of the infant-mother relationship. *Child Development*, 1969, 40 (4), pp. 969–1025.

Ainsworth, M.D.S., and Bell, S.M. Attachment, exploration, and separation: Illustrated by the behavior of one-year olds in a strange situation. *Child Development*, 1970, 41 (1), pp. 49–67.

Bayley, N., and Schaefer, E.S. Correlations of maternal and child behavior with the development of mental abilities: Data from the Berkeley Growth Study. *Monographs of the Society for Research in Child Development*, 1964, 29 (Serial No. 97).

Bell, S.M. The development of the concept of object as related to infant-mother attachment. *Child Development*, 1970, 41 (2), pp. 291–311.

Caldwell, B.M. What is the optimal learning environment for the young child? *American Journal of Orthopsychiatry*, 1967, 37, pp. 8–21.

Caldwell, B.M., Wright, C.M., Honig, A.B., and Tannenbaum, J. Infant day-care and attachment, *American Journal of Orthopsychiatry*, 1970, 40 (3), pp. 397–412.

Crandall, V.C., Preston, A., and Robson, A. Maternal reactions and development of independence and achievement behavior in young children. *Child Development*, 1960, 31, pp. 243–51.

Freeberg, N.E., and Payne, D.T. Parental influence on cognitive development in early childhood. A review. *Child Development*, 1967, 111, pp. 245–61.

Hess, R.D., and Shipman, V. Cognitive elements in maternal behavior. In J.P. Hill (ed.), *Minnesota Symposia on Child Psychology, Vol. I*. Minneapolis: University of Minnesota Press, 1967.

Hoffman, M.L. Power assertion by the parent and its impact on the child. *Child Development*, 1960, 31, pp. 899–911.

Honzik, M.P. Environmental correlates of mental growth. Prediction from the family setting at 21 months. *Child Development*, 1967, pp. 337–64.

Katkovsky, W., Preston, A., and Crandall, V.C. Parents' attitudes toward their personal achievements and toward the achievement behaviors of their children. *Journal of Genetic Psychology*, 1964, 104, pp. 105–21.

Mannino, F.V. Family factors related to school persistence. *Journal of Educational Sociology*, 1962, 35, pp. 193–202.

Moss, H.A., and Robson, K.S. Maternal influences in early social visual behavior. *Child Development*, 1968, 39, pp. 401–08.

Rubenstein, J. Maternal attentiveness and subsequent exploratory behavior of the infant. *Child Development*, 1967, 38, pp. 1089–1100.

Stoltz, L.M. Effects of maternal employment on children. *Child Development*, 1960, 31, pp. 749–82.

APPLICATION

These books are only a sample of the wide range of materials that are available for parents. Just because a book is listed here, don't take it as an endorsement. What works for you and your child is the best criterion for choosing any book or accepting any piece of advice.

Adler & Terry. *Your Overactive Child: Normal or Not?* Medcom ($6.95).

Apgar & Beck. *Is My Baby All Right?* Trident ($3.95).

Blaine, Jr. *Are Parents Bad for Children: Why the Modern American Family Is in Danger.* Coward, McCann, & Georghegan ($5.95).

Brazelton. *Infants and Mothers: Differences in Development.* Delta ($3.95).

Broadribb and Lee. *The Modern Parents' Guide to Baby and Child Care.* Lippincott ($10.00).

Brutten, Richardson, and Mangel. *Something's Wrong With My Child: A Parents' Book About Children with Learning Disabilities.* Harcourt Brace Jovanovich ($7.50).

Callahan. *The Working Mother.* Paperback Library ($0.95).

Caplan, ed. *The First Twelve Months: Your Baby's Growth Month by Month.* Grosset & Dunlap ($3.95).

Church. *Understanding Your Child From Birth to Three: A Guide to Your Child's Psychological Development.* Random House ($6.95).

Dreikurs and Cassel. *Discipline Without Tears: What to Do with Children Who Misbehave.* Hawthorn ($1.95).

Gerzon. *A Childhood for Every Child: The Politics of Parenthood.* Outerbridge & Lazard ($7.95).

Grey. *Discipline Without Tyranny: Child Training During the First Five Years.* Hawthorn ($4.95).

Karelitz. *When Your Child is Ill: A Guide to Infectious Disease in Childhood.* Warner Paperback Library ($1.75).

LeShan. *On "How Do Your Children Grow?"* Warner Paperback Library ($1.25).

LeShan. *How to Survive Parenthood.* Warner Paperback Library ($1.25).

Pomeranz and Schultz. *The First Five Years: A Relaxed Approach to Child Care.* Doubleday ($6.95).

Pryor. *Nursing Your Baby.* Pocket Books ($1.50).

Robertson and Wood. *Today's Child: A Modern Guide to Baby Care and Child Training.* Scribner's ($3.45).

Salk. *What Every Child Would Like His Parents to Know.* Warner Paperback Library ($1.50).

Shiller. *Childhood Illness: A Common Sense Approach.* Stein and Day ($7.95).

Smith. *The Encyclopedia of Baby and Child Care.* Prentice-Hall ($10.00).

Sparkman and Carmichael. *Blueprint for a Brighter Child.* McGraw-Hill ($5.95).

Steward and Olds. *Raising a Hyperactive Child.* Harper & Row ($8.95).

The Group for the Advancement of Psychiatry Committee on Public Education. *The Joys and Sorrows of Parenthood.* Scribner's ($5.95).

Wiener and Glick. *The Motherhood Book: Adventures in Pregnancy, Birth, and Being a Mother.* Macmillan ($2.95).

OTHER HUMAN DEVELOPMENT BOOKS

CHILDREN AND ADULTS: ACTIVITIES FOR GROWING TO-GETHER *by Joseph and Laurie Braga.* An imaginative collection of games, explorations, projects, and adventures that adults and children can do in the spirit of fun, helping each other to grow as they play together.

DEATH: THE FINAL STAGE OF GROWTH *by Elisabeth Kubler-Ross.* A powerful and emotional work by the renowned pioneer of the death and dying movement, giving new insights into the nature of death and its meaning as a key to our growth as human beings.

LEARNING AND GROWING: A GUIDE TO CHILD DEVELOPMENT *by Laurie and Joseph Braga.* Detailed descriptions of children's development from birth to age five, integrated with suggestions of activities to stimulate growth in the areas of motor, language, cognitive, and socioemotional development.

GROWING OLDER *by Margaret Hellie Huyck.* Filled with information, this optimistic view of aging explores the alternatives open to us that can add life to our years as well as years to our lives if we can break through the negative stereotypes our culture has about growing older.

GROWING WITH CHILDREN *by Joseph and Laurie Braga.* A sensitive and loving guide to understanding and meeting human needs shared by adults and children, examining the relationship between childhood experiences and adult behavior.

CULTURE AND HUMAN DEVELOPMENT *by Ashley Montagu.* A collection of unusual perspectives by this world-famous anthropologist and others, exploring the wide-ranging positive and negative effects humane and inhumane cultural and environment practices can have on developing human beings.